Collected
Poems

WILLIAM DUNLOP

CLASSIC DAY
PUBLISHING

Seattle, Washington
Portland, Oregon
Denver, Colorado
Vancouver, B.C.
Scottsdale, Arizona
Minneapolis, Minnesota

Classic Day Publishing
2925 Fairview Avenue East
Seattle, Washington 98102
877-728-8837
info@peanutbutterpublishing.com

TABLE OF CONTENTS

PREFACE

It makes me very happy to bring this book to its readers. First conceived as a very slim volume of William Dunlop's late poems, it steadily snowballed. Some very early poems handwritten in a small and tattered notebook surfaced, as it were, from his brother's attic. The very earliest were dictated to his older sister; he soon took over, writing in his own hand. They date from 1943-1946 (ages 7 to 10). Many show great promise; their volume shows, at least, indefatigable versifying. The chosen few appearing here reveal some early, and some lasting, influences and passions.

Most of this book consists of poems written in his maturity — early and otherwise. Nearly all of them appeared in *Caruso for the Children & Other Poems*, (Rose Alley Press, 1997) which is reprinted here almost in its entirety. Those that did not are placed in what I hope is rough chronological order.

A third section is a sampling of some *jeux d'esprit*. With his friend Hugh Brogan (they met as undergraduates at Cambridge) there developed a correspondence of many years in which they challenged each other to compose limericks and ghosts, which would distill a given work (opera, novel, epic, or merely some hapless human or god to its, or his, essence. The limericks and ghosts here are mostly William's. As for the Sprats — parodic variations on the nursery rhyme — Hugh gave *carte blanche* to include some of his in this book. Their initials denote authorship. Other Sprats, and other limericks, await publication.

Finally, to the late poems. He wrote to a friend, citing George Herbert's *The Flower*:

"And now in age I bud again,
    After so many deaths I live and write
        ....and relish versing"

After his retirement in 2001, in the last years of his life, he wrote, and revised, constantly. It was a wonderful outpouring: poems of astonishing variety and craftsmanship. Those which he finished are virtuoso pieces, reflecting, as has been said elsewhere, a lifetime of reading, writing, and performing poetry, novels and plays. Most importantly, to listening — to those, and to opera, and to the countless modulations of speech itself. These poems demand to be read aloud to hear their precise and musical cadences in the air, to catch the chime of their often subtly concealed rhymes, and to savor them on your tongue and in your ear.

Revelle Dunlop
Seattle, 2007

Childhood Poems

1943-1951

AET. 7-15

WILD ANIMALS

The panther as he crouches in the grass,
With his gooseberry eyes as pale as glass
The lion as he lies on the sandy ground,
Looks just like an earthy mound.

The tiger as he hides in the reeds,
With his eyes as smooth as beads
The wild hog as he runs o'er Deccan's Sandy Plain
Plunges on his mighty mane.

September 1943

THE MOOR

When I went upon the lea
Its many sights to hear and see
I went to where the Red Deer bounds
Listening for many sounds.

They too had much to see
As they were scared upon the lea
The lithe body of the weasel, and the hovering hawk
And even the stone chat's angry squawk.

And down by the cool clear bog
They were pursued by the barking dog
And when they climbed the rocky hill,
They looked into the valley stern and still.

The Royal Stag leader of the herd
Cared not for beast or bird
The quickest stag upon his feet,
Every hunter tried to get his meat.

And now the Royal Stag stands on high,
Watching the birds as they fly
And now to the stag a glass of ale
To bring an ending to my tale.

July 4, 1944

OUR CAT

Our cat sits by the fire all day,
And with her green eyes she looks so gay,
But she goes out into the dark of night
And with other cats she has a fight.

She looks so jolly sitting by the heat,
While the garden is full of sleet
It's almost uncanny how she crosses the street
And there is one thing she is very fond of — MEAT.

THE OLD CASTLE

Inside the empty moat was mud,
Left by some annual winter's flood
And the oaken castle door,
Gaunt, and grim, and wild, I saw.
Passing along by the stone wall
I came to a dining hall,
Where warriors rested after a fight,
And drank a health to their great might.

And then I came to the keep
Buried in everlasting sleep
It would have been a feeding place for a cat,
For it abounded with bat, mouse and rat.
I expected to feel a warrior's mailed hand,
And to hear his voice "Who goes there? Stand."
Then I walked away from the old keep
Letting it have its broken sleep.

December 1944

From THE YEAR

May
May, May, thou beautiful May
In thy fields the lambkins play
Every hot and cooling day
Is found in May

June
June, thou month of play
Thou holdest every lovely day
In thee mid-summer has its day
And June, thou art very gay

July
Thou hast the cooling showers
Strawberries and lovely flowers
And on the 5TH Hurrah! Hurrah!
That is my natal day.

COUNTRY SOUNDS

The crow of the cock as he welcomes the dawn
The sound of the child as he plays on the lawn
And the song of the birds of the morn
And the cry of the baby that's just been born

The sound of the grasshopper as he hides in the grass
The hum of the bee
The voice of the stranger as he goes pass
And sounds of what you see

The grunt of the pig in the farmyard stye
The bark of the farm yard dog
The song of the birds as they sing in the sky
And the cry of the water fowl in the bog

AN ASCENT OF BEN NEVIS

1. As we looked on that mountain so Noble and high
And saw the great peak that pierced the blue sky
And there were Eagles circling round
Making many an eerie sound

2. But then a thundercloud swiftly came
Drifting over that mountain of fame
And down came the rain pouring
No longer were the Eagles soaring

3. O'er us the rain held sway
We looked at each other and said "Not Today"
The next morning the sun rose in the mist
The thrill within me I could not resist

4. We packed the foods and coats and then away!
We formed a cavalcade so gay
Up we went on that rocky climb
At 8 o'clock on the chime

5. We put our coats on, it grew very cold
Below us there was a shepherd and fold
As noon grew nigh some food we took
And saw many an eagle's nook

6. And then we came to cold snow
And got a view of what was below
Far above us was the top
Where we would soon stop

7. We made a shelter of boughs
While the wind softly soughs
Next day we reached the top
Where we made a stop

8. Down we went from that mountain grand
At the bottom we made a stand
In the heart of the Cameron land
Brave mountain — brave men how grand!

December 27, 1944

JACK FROST

1. Jack Frost, he's a rascal as you know
He's the gardener's friend and foe
With frost he covers the ground
And makes every river icebound

2. Winter you have a rollicking son
Full of mirth and icy fun
With whiteness you cover the lawn
Which you see in the early dawn

PURITAN MEN

Part I
1. Charge, Oliver, Shoot, Oliver
Scatter the tyrants like grain
Work, Oliver, for England
Work shall not be in vain

2. Hampden, Eliot, and Pym
lend a helping hand
And any true Whig to-day
Follow the faithful band

3. Fairfax, Blake, and Deane
Help on land and sea
Remember those great men
In memory let them be

December 29, 1944

GAMES (Football and Cricket)

1. Of all games football is the best
The boys play it with zest
"Shoot"! "Hip, Hip, Hooray
Another goal for us to-day."

2. The summer game is cricket
In which you need bat, ball, and wicket
"Oh, lovely sir! there's a six"
"You've put their team in a lovely fix"!

MEALS

Breakfast
For Breakfast, we have Porridge and toast,
(We nether have anything roast),
I have toast with butter and marmite
Always spread fairly light.

Lunch
For the first course we have lots of things,
Some with four legs and some with wings,
And our puddings an awful Muddle,
I'd like to throw most of them in a puddle.

Tea
The nicest meal in the day is tea,
Bread-and-Butter starts of[f] you see,
And then biscuits, and jam and cakes,
Is the nicest thing for tea we make

Supper
I don't stay up with the rest,
That is confessed,
But before I go to bed,
With cereals and other things I am fed.

PURITAN MEN

Part II
1. At Chalgrove Field Hampden fell
Sad Puritan bells are ringing his knell
Fighting against the tyrant's band
Fighting for the liberty of his land

2. Among them all, Cromwell was the flower,
He ruled in work, truth, and power,
Oh, Oliver, remember that great day,
At Marston Moor, the turning-point in sway.

3. Blake, there master of the water,
Making England the sea's eldest daughter,
Here comes Van Tromp with his broom,
And above us the Dutch ships loom.

January 1, 1945

AT THE CORNER

At the corner look left and right
Every day and every night
Or you'll be run over by a car
Safety First is better by far

THE BIRDS

1. The Magpie, Rook, and Crow
All over England go
With its sweet song the Nightingale
Is heard in many a lovely vale

2. And the mighty Eagle King
For his delight the birds sing
And the Falcon, Hawk, and Owl
And the tame Common Fowl

3. Birds of the air, caw and sing
Your world is a different thing
Tiny Songsters lift your notes
And fly in your coloured coats

4. From Great Eagle to tiny Wren
Do not despise men
We are happy on earth
Where God Almighty gave us birth

THE WIND

O Wind, thou howlest through the trees
Thou givest a great gale and a gentle breeze
Sometimes you make a Hurricane
And Sometimes in a calm you'r[e] held in chain

THE TUDOR LINE
History 1485-1714

1. Henry VII
Richard III was killed at Bosworth
And that to the Tudor line gave birth
For 24 years Henry sat on the throne
And was directed by the Church of Rome

2. Henry VIII
As Henry the VIIII had a great love for gold
Against the Church he was very bold
He destroyed the monasteries you know
And became the Pope's bitter foe

3. Edward and Mary
Edward reigned from 1547 to '53
And reigned for 6 years you see
Mary got the help of Spain
To get rid of the Protestants, but it was in vain

4. Elizabeth
Elizabeth had sailors, like Drake and Howard,
And they beat the Spanish cowards
Drake sailed to the new world again and again
Every time strafing the will of Spain

THE DEATH OF CROMWELL

1. I see before me a sick-bed lie
On it a man is ready to die.
He has rode into battle again and again
But illness has broken that iron frame

2. Look at the date, it's September 3rd
And I have often heard
Of Worcester and Dunbar
Its Oliver, heard of afar

3. Lord of England Farewell!
Soon the bells will be ringing thy knell
Think of Naseby and of Rowton Heath
Oliver Cromwell, the Country's Relief

TO MY FATHER

I remember happy days
Before this war and after
When the house rang with praise
And was full of happy laughter

[1945]

RIVER BOATS

1. Boats go a-sailing, up river, down river,
Boats go a-sailing all day long.
The Ganges and the Gaudalquivir,
Keep to themselves the boatman's song.

2. Boats go a-sailing, white and black
Now steamers go a-steaming, big as a whale
But when you've forgotten, nought can bring back,
The recollection of a good day's sail.

3. It's only patience that keeps your theme,
Going on still, rage as you may,
When you're becalmed on the mid-stream
With the sun beating down on you, on a wind-less day

September 8, 1946

INNELLAN

Dim years ago, when all the world
Was young and strange and innocent,
When tears came soon — as soon forgot —
And days were quickened with content,
For three delicious weeks my world
Was centred round the little town
Twixt Toward Keep and gay Dunoon,
A world of burns and heather hills
And sweeter memories faint and vague
That made the world a paradise
From Gourock Pier to Ailsa Craig!
Swift rushing streams and rock-strewn shores
And Arran's mountains blue and far
And nearer, greener, kindlier hills —
These were my joys; and when the star
Of earliest evening overshone,
Then I, more rich than any prince
Would scamper homeward up the hill
And then — such beauty not seen since —
Soon darker, bluer grew the sky
(while solemn-eyed I sat at tea)
And many-hued the hills around,
And many-hued the sea.

December 18, 1951

Poems

1958-1997

DA CAPO

Barred from the garden, made to scrub my hands,
Sulky, but not yet prompted to rebel,
My straining fingers half an octave spanned.
Father, seduced by feminine persuasion,
Had paid my fees, installed a Baby Grand.

Yet, wise in my predestined generation
(Promised an apple if I practised well)
I glimpsed the serpent in the treble clef,
Unlike my mother, grasped the implication,
Read his contorted signature aright;
Born to this conflict forking black and white.

Initial bars, though sharp with overtone,
Engaged no accidental quest:
Five fingers yearning bone to bone,
My heart a faltering metronome,
Bone of my bone I struck, depressed.

I modulate from stage to stage,
Pounding by treadmill scales to death —
My erring parents taxed my breath
Mortgaged my garden heritage.

A WREATH FOR JIMMY

(Second Lieutenant James Dunlop, The Royal Scots:
Killed in action at Hong Kong, December 1941)

I

There's that last snapshot of us all together,
I have it still, somewhere.
Beneath the sharp Glengarry, your taut stare
Scorning the blindfold: Mother's sad endeavour
To engineer a smile, or look serene —
She fails at both. I, four years old, a boy
Still half a baby, bump her knee, act coy;
Father's anxiously proud, and ranged between,
Our sisters and our brother stand
Gawky, and awkward at your being so grand.

II

Another one: this time of you alone
In profile, oddly pale,
Against the front French windows. Yet
Not quite alone, for sharply, at the edge,
Your black reflection scouts the milky pane.
One day, long after, Father held it up
Close to his eyes: I heard the Celtic slur
Half-trip his tongue: "We should have known.
See the dark fellow. Aye, aye, we should have known."
The phone-bell keened.
He laid you down — face down — and then
Became the brusque hard-headed doctor once again.

III

A curious day that December —
Everyone started to cry
All over the house: I remember
I wanted so much to know why.
I peeped round the door at our brother —
He bawled "Go away!" between sobs;
I started to seek out my mother,
But my hand fell short of the knob...
Hong Kong, Hong Kong, what a silly song
To sing in one's head all the time;
Hong Kong, Hong Kong, that's where I belong
In the sense of a nonsense rhyme.

IV

Dear Jimmy:
            Why I call you "dear"
Is something of a problem; it's not clear
If what I feel's a due affection, or
A selfish hope of what I'm looking for
Inside myself. Remember, I was only four
— And you were only twenty.
Yet, when I was still a baby, very apt to cry
For no good reason, you could hush my squalls
Better than anyone, I'm told. And I recall
Just the one image of us all —
A kind of ritual. You elder four would ride
Your bikes — *you* leading — round and round the drive;
I, on my scooter, scamped along behind.
That chain of children circles in my mind.
Is that a clue to what I need to find?

V

I wonder how we'd get along together, you and I?
I seem to share your taste in books,
But lack the painter's eye.
I think we're much alike in looks,
You're better dressed, though... I forgot:
You've little use for reading now,
Maintain a white unwrinkled brow,
Eyes, once more blue than mine, are...

And all your wardrobe's out at pocket!

VI

By getting killed, you killed our mother. It took years.
I didn't see her toughness, just her tears
At unaccountable moments, and grew cunning
At skipping off the times I saw them coming.
I'd hear her pause in rummaging upstairs...
Your things. I knew. But had my own affairs.
Once she was crouching in the darkened basement.
You were the first-born. I was no replacement.

No crime in that. And no forgiveness either.

VII

No bugle, not a muffled drum
Beat to accompany her home.
No martial men, with arms reversed,
Mounted no escort to her hearse.
No ceremonial's cannon's roar
Induced ironic doves to soar.
The day she claimed the soldier's grave
Her heart was set on, nothing gave
My eyes a hint how to behave —
I found it easy to be brave

Seeing a book by Bergson, *Laughter*,
Laid by her bedside, after
The cremation. It was rather rushed.
She took too many pills. But that was…?

Hush.

VIII

But what I think of is our neighbor's wife —
Remember her? — smart, sporty, full of life? —
Threw avid glances at me, burst out, crying:
"God! don't you realise your mother's *dying*?"
I did, and shook her off. Went for a walk
Down frosted roads which gleamed as white as chalk
Until I reached the lake — a favorite place
Of yours, I shouldn't wonder. Ice fringed, like coffin lace,
The shiny black inertness of its face.
Clocks chimed. The last street-lamps went out.
No moon, but stars were tingling all about.
I must have sat there hours, quite still, except when, once or twice,
I cast a listless stone that broke no ice.
You, she were stars. But I was set apart.
My eyes were stones. And ice, all ice, my heart.

IX

And this I grudge you: that thimbleful of dust
You have about you somewhere; love I must
And cannot, brother. Wasn't there enough
For all of us? Where does one get the stuff
Except by being born in time? You were.
Brother, I'm older than you ever were!
Hers cracked, broke slowly; yours was rash
And cast away its substance in a flash —
Where to? — the love you'd barely time to start
To spend?
        O my dead brother, give me your live heart!

DEPARTURE

True to parole, the lover never misses
The train the independent fail to catch;
His careful schedule for a clean dispatch
Constrains his mind
To keep control on would-be deeding kisses:
Both trust their lips no more than commonplaces,
Recheck their watches, synchronise their faces,
Let hands unwind.

Grief is outbid by ritual, regulations,
The private rules framed for two-handed bluff,
When just to cut one's losses is enough
To count as gain
By their contrived, unstable computations,
The falsehoods both refuse to realise,
Until the rain unlinks him from her eyes,
Blind as his streaming pane.

TWENTY-ONE

For you this random date holds special meaning,
An individual day, whose implications
Of fresh prerogatives involve a figure
Which featured large in recent calculations.

But you may ask, beset by disillusion,
Classing yourself as adult long before:
"Why wait to recognise the finished product?
Can this one year improve upon my score?

Convention underlines a simple number
Significant to none but bleared tradition."
But you should feel, by virtue of being human,
The power and worth of human superstition.

Maintain the child's perception and response,
Which adult industry too soon encumbers,
Defy analysis, let fancy play
With charms, red-letter days, and lucky numbers.

Let birds be auguries, the Zodiac wise;
Let curious ciphers fade to mere statistics
Thirteen should be ill-omened, Christmas keep
Its twelfth-night ritual, three above all be mystic.

Divinities and legend haunt each total;
Seven should indicate good luck, imply
In your new age a potent magic whence
All mystery and fortune multiply.

ROMANCE

France holds your affections, Italy mine;
History repeats itself — at least we may
Adopt our preference as stage or backcloth,
Act the Magnificent or Roi Soleil;
Or, since no unities confine our play,
Make Rome and Gaul our new denominators,
Their swaying fortunes map out our design
Performed in private by the two translators.

My trampling legions overrun your acres,
You, in due time, besiege and sack my city;
We take our cues for donning bays or sackcloth,
Our scripts are tragic, our impromptus witty,
So we can dramatise and purge the pity
Of past relations, but we act in vain:
Between us still, impassive as spectators,
The icy barriers of the Alps remain —
Since we in our more recent, distant days
Distorted one bold language separate ways.

CLAIR DE LUNE

Full on my unsleeping face
The moon squints down and stares
At dirty plates, and discs, and books,
The sum of my affairs.

Through moving boughs and fidget leaves
The moonbeams pick their way and sift
Into my room, and there freeze up
And stabilise the ruck and drift.

Where sunlit diagrams made play
With tremulous and graded tread,
The hard cold glare impels the trees
To rivet patterns round my head,

And holds the quaking mazes firm
A concrete flux of marbled light,
Inconstant swirl of teacup dregs
At variance with second sight.

The shadows stick to one dimension:
The moon has sucked all colour dry,
And squares each circle, rules each line,
But will not trick the aching eye

By rounding out the taut-drawn blankets
Flat by my unharboured side,
Expands the waste of sheeted void
And blanches my imagined bride.

Controls my pillow's pied confusion,
Allows no fleeting leafcast trace
Of eyebrow curve, or lovelock curling,
Or lightning-sketched unconscious face.

Lays bare and sharp unshuttered lies,
And proves, not makes, my nights insane;
When moonbeams dazzle through my eyes
To pierce my disappointed brain.

LANDSCAPE, WITH LOVERS

All night the wind pursued its strong intentions,
Surfing the hair, and flexing tightened eyes;
It shook the heaving curtains out of stupor,
And rolled its cloudy backcloth round the sky.

High in the woods the yawning trees reshuffle,
Their trunks rough-muscled and compact like bears;
Streams tight as drums jostle their banks descending
In schoolboy mêlée clattering downstairs.

In this clear hour when wind and clouds decamp
Each sight and sound snaps briskly into place;
Lovers find certainty, and deftness in translating
The complications of each other's face.

The sunlight joins their hands, evolves the sharp
Emphatic portent of a settled vane
Which points unfaltering towards fair weather,
As confident as larksong after rain.

Her eyes admit this bright invasion, deepen
To share her heart's enlargement, and perceive
Her lover's tenderness worn like a halo,
His heart conspicuous on a tranquil sleeve.

EXPOSURE

The girl of flesh with nimble ways
Plays sister to the girl of stone,
Coquettes with sculptured brows and curls
And twines with marble arms her own.

I, with my camera alert,
Should warm to only one of these;
Reject the frankly static thighs
For skirted and imagined knees.

The loins that narrow to no sense
Have no stone maidenhead to lose;
The other, should she profit there,
Is purse-proud, and may yet refuse.

Ingenious art on this conferred
The symmetry and form of grace;
Imagination wrought, conceived
The mute perfection of the face.

The sculptor's hand ennobled stone:
No hands or brain of worth conspired
To model flesh; the cause alone,
And not the end, was lust-inspired.

I roll the next film on while she
Disengages, gaily prances
Across the grass to talk of tea,
And gathering clouds, and future dances.

Nothing of her could stand or stay;
No thing in her is permanent
Except my snaps, which will not grant
A hope of real development.

No darkroom touch can souls enlarge;
No chance, at least, that I'll be shewn
A cause for preference between
The girls of celluloid and stone.

GRASS WIDOW

She must have been
All loveliness when young, her pride
Remains that of a girl admired,
Elected queen
By benefit of beauty; as a bride
Inheriting by right all she desired.

She had no cause
To foster practical or homely traits,
Spin subterfuge to shade less pleasing features.
Born to applause,
Even her most capricious moods won praise:
Fey, inconsistent, fascinating creature!

Her charm still wins:
Breaches of common etiquette or taste
Are unrelated to her giant inconsequence;
Wreathed with stale smoke, and odorous with gin,
Her lips drop jewels, half genuine, half paste,
Poke equal fun at lust and innocence.

She knows her friends —
Eunuchs and whores, the decadent but witty,
Never the soberly respectable, discreet,
Who would not comprehend
The sudden urge to shock, delight a city
By hopping breathless through the public street.

Mark Antony comes after.
But now, just slightly drunk, superb in cloths
Quite ludicrous on others, she expounds the span
Of years of laughter:
Enchanting child, nymph of the Cyprian groves,
And mistress of each strong, successful man.

BEDTIME STORY

Once on a time, and long ago,
No crowsfeet stalked across the snow
That charmed the sullen soil below.

Then full-cheeked berries sparkled red
That black and shrunk hang overhead;
Hearts were unscathed, though fingers bled.

The dwarfs are dead, or very old,
The fire is low, the tale is told;
Snow is less magical than cold.

No witches plot behind our backs
Hunched over rents or income tax:
The unconsulted mirror cracks.

Only the tales themselves stay young,
As now our gauche indulgent laughter
Fades, like enchantment, from the tongue.

What can they mean by "ever after"?

VENUS DE MILO

Her perfect measurements, the faultless line
Of bust and buttock subtly contradict
Their female emphasis: statistics lie,
And art eschews too much. No human flaw
Or blemish other than the waves inflict
Exists to indicate she offers more

Than scars, truncated arms, which serve to make her
Silly enough for us to tolerate
That arrogance, unsoftened by the breakers,
Which holds her public in supreme contempt
— Which they return: we scorn, but cannot hate
Milord in shirt-tails, exquisites unkempt.

Around her, all day long, there drifts and swirls
The changing crowd, and each new tide contains
Men with attractive and imperfect girls
Who count her favours not worth their possessing
And ebb away, nor care if Venus deigns
To grant her impotent and frigid blessing.

VESPERS

"All that calm Sunday that goes on and on
And earth is but a star, that once had shone."
– James Elroy Flecker

Osteopaths despair of Sundays;
At worst, all other days will tap
Or hobble by in splints, on crutches.
Sunday's a state and not a progress: sap
And marrow stultify, dissolve. The light
Prolongs a quivering bonelessness, a gap.

At dusk, a mess of bells
Litter the wind, eddy, clog up the drains
With shreds of antique placarding, and still
Their hollow gravity airs its refrain:
The warder's tattered drum, whose menace guides
A shabby cortege fumbling through the rain.

Nothing so bold as being shot down in flames
Attends the final wizened lapse of day:
Light just subsides, untidy, uneventful
As Sunday papers rumpled, thrust away,
The leprous bed whose stale commotion now
Dwindles to chaos, uniform and grey.

An irresponsible, warped view? Perhaps.
But apathy is hardest to survive;
And "this calm Sunday that goes on and on"
Is rancid energy, looks to deprive
New generations of all creeds to die for,
Or of a better way to keep alive.

INTRUSION

I sit between the window and the light:
My shadow looks back through the pane
Returning stare for stare; again
I bend my head and wit to write.

Forgetting my dark image keeps
His station in the glass, intent
On mirroring each filament
Of hair the lamplight deftly steeps,

And drowning in its oily sheen
My shadowed face. I lift my hand
And, startled, glimpse that curt unplanned
Manoeuvre reproduced on screen.

All that my mind or hand distorts
This faithfully reciprocates,
Now two poised pens, ten fingers wait
In grave attendance on my thought,

Two outward selves grimace or grin
And bow to partner: doubled odds
Beat down with customary rods
The frettings of the self within

Which, master still, still hesitates
To draw the curtains, loose the catch,
Or move away, and so dispatch
The creature of his long debate.

For spasms of impatient rage
Impel no bullet through the brain:
The neat abrasion of a pane
Tinkles the flickering page,

A poem skimmed, lines left for dead,
Paper as glossy and as blank
As when this window cups the dank
Infected hush of light unshed.

SPRING IN NOTTING DALE

Week-end. A negro springheels by; the breeze
Puffs out his sunflower shirt.
                              Too fine
Too soon? — a whiff of orchards still
Clings to the pastoral adage; there they fear
One night may wrench their blossoming quilt away
And freeze their fingers. Here, our more
Complex, new-fangled, urban lore applies
The phrase, with shades of meaning. Here,
A hot blight's what we're scared of, here
Sun flicks a yellow duster, slates seem
To glitter brightest when they give off steam.

Fever, not frost, impends. The hot-with-jaundice eye
Is our potential killer. Here, in quarantine,
The children play apart, the cream
Façade flakes sour, and iron buds
Of railings stab at the diminished hues
Of what they isolate, a few
Sad knots of ailing daffodils around
The sooty trunks, and blackening tin-cans.

Next-door, old fifty-nine,
(Here no one's 'neighbour') sports
A brand new lemon door; knob, knocker, number
Tricked out in jet
                    — you see his ads
Flyblown in sweetshop cases,
NO COLOURED — spidery
On yellowing cards.
                    KEEP BRITAIN WHITE
His windows mouth at me; I watch
Two long leg sheer delight black nylon girls
Accost a ginger cat, to scratch
His sharp ecstatic chin. They move on, smartish,
Palming their skirts, prim roses...
                              Now! the sun
Breaks through on them, flares into stalls where brass
Glints at mahogany; where rich-as-rum
Jamaican voices, husky dusky hands
Fondle big grapefruit, hold debate,
Wanting to now how much: cheaper today...

Marvellously, in-
and-out the ochre chimney-stacks
That fringe my view,
Jinks the one swallow which alone won't make
More than a breath of summer, but where that
Most breeds and haunts, may woo
Our gentler senses here to cultivate
A less capricious sun, a warmth
More general, air that's delicate.

THE TREE-RIDER

He was the greenstain boy with barky knees
and heart yo-yoing between throat and boots,
crouched in the highest saddle of a tree

the wind was wild to pluck up by the roots
and whip cartwheeling up into a sky
flustered with clouds like floundering parachutes.

For all its rant and mime of agony,
the tree had stuck its toes in, bobbed and weaved,
a crooked angler all agog to try

to wrap the gale up in its trawl of leaves.
He, at his point of balance, eyes slashed wide,
cheered wind and wood alike, rode the big heaves,

the thresh and bulge, the pulse he sat astride
which was the place, but more a way to be —
you cannot say that he identified

with blast or root, the founded or the free.
From their long grapple neither could decide
he learnt the style of not being satisfied,
a point to perch on, his identity.

WIMBORNE MINSTER

There, on our way to Devon and the sea,
We stopped for lunch. The hulking Minster lay
Bemused by sun, and all the town, that day,
Yellow and soggy, like a pear, with heat.
My father shivers, pushes back his plate,

And freezes Wimborne Minster.
An apple core,
A fox's mask, a dead tobacco smell....
The doves brew silence, and a mellow bell
Burdens the air, beats twice. Life, life is short.
Outside, my father lifts a hand to tilt

The brightness from his eyes.
Whom should I meet
In Wimborne Minster, if I went there now,
With just that slant of shadow on his brow?

My father cursed the winding coast-road. We
Were on our way to Devon, and the sea.

ONE SEPTEMBER SUNDAY
(3 September 1939)

Lace curtains billow outwards, try to drape him.
His ladder's jammed against the sill. Indoors,
Somebody's left the wireless on: it drifts his way
Thinned to warm air. All talk, no do. He draws
His brush along the lintel square and solid,
And cocks his head and aims the next clean swathe.
The radio goes on murmuring to itself
Like some sick, sad old man....Here goes:
Fresh crimson trim. How bloody stiff he'll be
Tomorrow, God knows; and his nails get clogged
Keeping his hand in. But, in such fair weather —
Sun feathering his back, the way the wind blows —
He loves the work. He wouldn't trade this job.
He'd like to see the painter who'd do better.

MIDLAND AUTUMN

The old house, freshly whitewashed
to make a dying splash,
briefly blood-spattered,
as its last mountain-ash
breaks out in a rash skitter.

Along the curb range
ochre and orange
cars, a ruddy lorry, vans:
one buffer's lemon sponge
rubs up a richer bronze.

Beyond, drab muddy fields:
a brandnew, bandbox yellow
tractor cuts a bold
shadow across the furrows.
Behind, a swell of sallow

woods, hooded in smoky
duns, wan tans.
The sky's turned raw and streaky
where the pines aim to spike
the sun's cold yolk.

Homeward bob crimson shopping-
bags; boys in brilliant blazers,
redbreasted, whistling; Mrs. Croft's mop
of tawny hair; Jane's russet scarf; the Major's
breast plugged with a shocking poppy.

SOUTHAMPTON: 1940

Just such a September —
the flushed air of evening; the blue mist curling
and wreathing the tree-trunks, furling the leaves;
the first star sharp as a pin by the inky steeple.
Black water heaving
sluggish, like oil, in its lip, and suck,
at piling and shipway and jetty;
and the black felt city
over the river, cut close to the sky, breathing
a feathery hush; and the west amazing —
not the freakish blazing
of one night, or two; but all through
just such a September.

How late it stayed light!
— Of so sanguine a timbre,
the sailor's delight
of red sky at nightfall, the jutty
steeple and chimney, the hulk of the city,
and the black river.
And the humming, the throbbing,
not splitting, but brimming
the quiet with their quiet persistence in coming
night after night in the gloaming,
like flock on black flock of the homing
geese, serene, precise,
and in such numbers!
Not five in formation, not fifty,
but the five hundred
German bombers —

The red sky at midnight! The clamor!

BESIDE THE SEASIDE

You wouldn't say that she "submitted." No,
Whatever prompted her was something new
and docile not at all. Perhaps it had to do
with the short turf, the white cliff edge, the slow
cloud promenade, the surge and thud below

as each fresh wave broke down. So, anyway,
touch, tremor, nakedness all made good sense
to her, quite suddenly, and down she lay
and smiled, and helped him to forget the tense
first panic, meeting not the least defense.

And afterwards, she begged a cigarette,
lazed on her back, and beamed back at the blue
sky, blameless. He was dumb. More vehement yet
the sea beat up against the cliffs, and threw
its whopping slogs into a cave that drew

the sinewed swell out of a foaming sleeve
and sucked it in, to — like one heaving block
of quartz — explode: boom hollowly; and leave
in skittery files licksplittling through the rocks,
till the next wave recruited them, and shocked

itself to spume, finding passivity
exceeded penetration. He watched (while she
lay with her skirt around her hips, and smiled
as at a dutiful, obliging child)
and felt the strangest pity for the sea.

GOING WEST

After the black Atlantic, America blazes:
a gold web of coast-roads, pendants and clusters
of valuable towns, the brilliant traces of Boston
falling behind, New York approaching....
Who would think black-out, except
a child of the 'forties, who sips
quick at his drink, hoods the flame of his lighter's
pinch of illumination?

He used to turn chairs into ships; he was sometimes a car,
a puffer-train often: all peaceable transformations,
pile-ups and crashes and wrecks notwithstanding.
But his flights were always a bomber's;
the cities he built were strictly viewed from above,
and marked for destruction. He croons
as the clenched hand coasts over
in a long loving arc, and pinkly unfurls
on target, releases blockbusters.

Poum! he implodes, and coughs, to persuade his neighbor,
or convert himself. A gunmetal voice
desires he extinguish
his smoke. He sits to attention,
cradles briefcase to paunch, settles his glasses;
his hair's thinning out, he's nearing his forties.

Watch out, New York: take cover, Boston.
A child of the 'forties is now
the man of the world.
Wheee...he confides to his cup, and *ka-pow!*
Before he unbuckles his seatbelt,
he should brush the bombs from his hands.

IN MONTANA

My tenth day in America, I found
the place became less funny. Nothing changed:
our Greyhound lapped the miles reflectively,
and still we ran beside the railroad track
which bore us company, from long time back,
into a future looking just as blank.

Any old novelty thus came to count
for something special. The spare earth moved to sleekness,
as freshly fledged, beneath a combing wind,
as the first green in Eden. Once or twice
we passed a shack still flaking off its hinges,
or, in the roadside lurch, a baking car
whose driver had baled out God only knows
how long ago, and left his '50 Olds
marooned in time. I'd never seen the grass
look just that new, or relicts quite as ageless.

My eyes were being widened. When I saw
a big fresh sign *Historical Monument:*
1900 point to vacant distance
I hardly raised a smile: I looked out, sharper,
to be in time for what was there to see.

A FACE IN THE CROWD

Who does she remind me of,
That girl? — eyes dark, black hair
With blacker sheen, cut square,
A Sphinx-like look, a Pharaoh's daughter
— And with that thought my memory's caught her,
I almost call out "Clare!"

And she responds, but with a shrug
That says I've stared enough,
Then bends to flick a pinch of fluff
Disdainfully away;
Clare's coat was never such a grey,
Nor of such modish stuff.

And yet, for just a month or so,
Ten years ago, her being slim
And smiling, set my heart askim —
And with that thought sweeps in a flood
Of curious pain, as when the blood
Regarrisons a limb

Or merely, as now, fires a blush
To think how, while the sun ran hay-
Wire through her hair, I lay
Demurely at her side, to trace
Her dusky Cleopatra face
Till pyramids decay —

My very thought, my own cliché...
Ingenuous as I was! But soon
Knew better. She was not to blame
As I recall. I wonder how I came
To call her back to mind? Or met
This tiny rankling of regret,
This milligram of shame?

LESSONS ON THE LAWN

Squirrels will never learn, insist
on treating serious humanists

with active, unconcealed suspicion.
To make them query their tradition,

pacifically I offered one
part of an old and nasty bun,

and wore my pal-to-squirrels grin.
Across the grass he skeetered, in

a series of electric shocks:
tail flexed, pop-eyed, he stopped to box

the air, as signal I should lob
what I might have to stop his gob

and, when it fell six inches short,
he glared, and quivered; sniffed, and thought,

and made a dash for it, and bolted
booty in cheek. I felt insulted

by his off-hand manipulation.
Squirrels lack discrimination,

where we distinguish. Proof: I wouldn't
dispense stale crumbs to bug-eyed students.

SINGLE MINDED

"Well," I say —
For the third time—as pauses
Lengthen, like the shadows outside,
"I'd better be off...." — but I stay
For that one last drink, and savor
How he's getting fatter,
And sip at her prettiness: though, of course, I'd
Want something better.

"Please don't trouble...." I say, but they have
To come to the gate,
Though it's turning colder.
And I turn, at the end of the street,
For my casual, obligatory wave
Just as she snuggles her head
On his chest, and his arm rounds her shoulder.

Not that I'm envious! "Poor chap"
(I was bound to say) "one saw it coming:
Still, he could do much worse."
And I — think of those all set to come running;
Am I sorry I didn't...?
Just the reverse.

Yet I see them still, as I round the corner,
In the same attitude
And the kiss uncompleted; she lifting her face
As he moves to secure her
In the way man and wife
Flowing back to each other, may turn to exclude
Mere acquaintance from their life.

"Do come again!" she said brightly,
And he chimed, "Any time...."
I might, I suppose, but it's not very likely....
Could they entertain
All my thirstiness? No —
Though not seeking to slight them —
I won't go again.
Until we can invite them.

THE PHOENIX

One flesh, both birds, we stoop. Claws
Pluck at our nape. Who kills, who dies?
In a warm rain
Of feathers, plummeting, I see her eyes
Strain at a favorite surprise
And melt. Flex of her craning neck
Seems set to drain
All savor from the air; a beak
That's soft as flannel delves
Deep, to my very quick. Our pulses stall, and pause.
Clock ticks again. A chink
Of light wanes on her forehead, and we blink
Back to a recollection of ourselves.

A real thrush chirps, outside. O
Fond allusions, lucid similes
Of fowl, and fire,
You lose your relevance, not by degrees,
But in one throb. She says, "You'll freeze...."
And sheets us deftly, as if dead;
Yes: to desire.
One man, one woman, in one bed;
All wooden, now. My lips,
Still mumbling on a random curl, let go.
It leaves an ashen taste.
She sighs, and shifts. I find my hand displaced.
Her mouth looks sooty, charred by the eclipse

Which yet is only passing.
                                        Glints
Again, like an awakened eye,
A flaring disc
To play along the curving of her thigh
— That lissom tinder — and supply
A sheen of plumage to the badge
Of nestling down.
Light widens, bridges us, to pledge
And burnish, in our blending,
The sudden bird who, in one strut, will rinse
Lethargy from his wings.
The sparks dance on our throats; he starts to sing
In one unbroken melody, ascending.

VARIANTS OF LOVE

At home, the great philanthropist forgets
His children's birthdays, and confuses names;
Sometimes his study window, shooting up,
Will bellow briefly at their noisier games —
They see his picture in the papers, awed
Beyond laughter that they know he snores.

He brings a book to meals. The children poke
And mutter urgently, buzz like pent flies,
Stare glumly at his incidental jokes:
Their faces pass like motes before his eyes.
Once, a bread-pellet, right off target, burst
Full on his cheek: his hand dismissed the wasp.

But this is the great man: Peace Prize,
Humanitarian, champion of the poor...
And Mozart, too, rapt with his string quartet
(D Minor) while Constanze strove to bear —
"Engage a wet-nurse? Bring him up on water!"
(K. 421.) The child died two months later.

I honor one, and love the other, take
All my best girls to hear *The Magic Flute*
And Universal Love; I load them each
In turn with Pamina's attributes,
And fail to gauge their own. I draw
Away from one to love another more —

Or so I fool myself. Admit it, then, I lack
That seeming distance from my own that tells
Of wider sympathies; but still my heart
Beats time at odds with those engaging bells
Which chime for harmony, to cherish one
And let the rest lapse into dead-and-gone.

And yet, between two stools, I value most
Those individual hands which ease my falls
And try to raise me to them; being so close
To two or three shields me from loving all
In my apartness: that music Mozart tried
To sing himself to rest with, as he died.

WORDS IN THE NIGHT

Night, and hearing
Makes sense again; the air is clearing
And the small sounds sharpen, like stones
Dropped in the snow, which, disappearing,
Still pettily dint
That fragile composure, but by it
Made pertinent.

So words in the night
Fracture the stillness, and enhance it
Along with themselves, as black and white
Bring out the quality in each other,
And the intervening
Silence in speech should discover
An intenser meaning.

Now I could speak
So clear that each syllable would be telling
Tales of the heart; and hear,
As you pause in reply, the silence spelling
Out love, receiving
All the phrases of joy from the mere
Dear sound of your breathing.

But all I am saying
Is: *Isn't it quiet?* — and the words conveying
Far and wide, and no more
Than the howl of a dog compulsively baying
Under the sway of the moon;
Or the blab of the tap; or a far clock striking
The same jumbled chime as at noon.

LOVE DUET

Some — I believe it — find this most pleasing fiction
the stuff of truth: a voice that pulses
conveys the strains of spirit *in excelsis,*
the full heart's purest diction;
and when the strings squeal loudest, brass bombardment thunders,
true love, they moan, and on that top note founder.

I like it, too, but in a dubious fashion:
great gulps of airs that I sup up inflate
the body's currency; at such high rates,
the poor heart pitches to contrary motions,
churns blood to borscht, and canonizes hormones,
and bellows bravos at its own performance.

And so, my love, switch off that braggart tenor
plighting his troth in full fidelity,
that shrill soprano's billowing high sea
of outrage offered her ambiguous honor —
I love them both, indeed, but to distraction:
your being here concerns my satisfaction.

Love moves by subtler rhythms, and small sounds:
a glass set down, clothes shucked, skins' conversation,
duet of breaths — the orchestration's
conventional enough, but it abounds
in touches of a sheer felicity: catch
in my voice; your chuckle; a struck match.

SILENCES

Some stress the cant of an eyebrow when lovers entirely
accept that each comprehend the other,
but *not*...let us say, her favorite show on the telly,
his Worcestershire sauce, reproduction of Whistler's mother —

unaccountable! And soon, laughing matters. Other pauses
                                        seem simpler:
for instance, it's evening. The normal windows are open.
The view from our room proposes a modest sampler
of backyards and roofs, some appletrees, green hills sloping

away to range vaguely the usual blue mountains beyond.
The sky is mottled with clouds like dangerous bruises.
A blubbering faucet, some child's cry add mites of sound
to the brim of silence summing us up, and our noises,

while the sun simply goes down. We may not lie to
each other, we know this: we are dumb in each other's distress
at all that we share, but would rather not try to,
are not equipped to express.

END OF SUMMER: After Yasujiro Ozu

September's here: so what. Trees
Stand sulky, without breeze to shake
The dust from their soured green. The lake
Stays creased, has lost the shimmer
It's worn all summer.
Wasps are a bugger, and the days-old papers
That bat them off report that rape
Is on the rise. A favorite cup
Dives at the kitchen floor. Both pennants are wrapped up.

And grandparents have come, to stay,
Fret, get in the way,
And bribe the kids to know them better.
My wife looks out a tighter sweater
And aims her sharp-edged breasts her mother's way.
Grandfather scores
Our age's laxity, deplores
Disorder. I tell him I hate barbers.
And conversation lapses
                        and all strength is labor.

The children tire, and quarrel, and are pecked,
Too late, to bed. My wife subjects
The nylons she peels off to scrutiny
That has no eyes for me.
We lie, apart, in bed
And hear stray peevish buzzes overhead
And know they talk of us. "You can tell...."
They're taking turns to say, "...not going well...."
And "*I* would say...." and "That's what *I* said."

Ozu would show them smooth worn kimonos,
Squat on their heels, compose
Their hands, and in their silence frame
Words which remain unspoken. All of us would choose
A mode of anguish kinder on the eye:
The rest is all the same
At heart, at least. At least, we try
To live, and fail, at least.
I slide a hand. She clenches up her thigh.
What goes to make a man makes me a beast...?

I climb from bed, and look toward the lake:
A strand of willow prints
Its slender patterns darker on the dark
That keeps the mountain — Fuji, or Rainier? —
Away till dawn restores to it the tints
It's worn for ages. I can hear
The whole house fill up with the quiet breathing
Of old, and young, even
Hers, at last. And now, still later,
The moon spreads out her fan across the water.

IN EXTENUATION

Mankind on trial: yes, it might melt the stones
to hear poor Nature's tales of rape and sack,
the tears wrung from her since we relish salt.
We lay our belt across Alaska's back?
Guilty. But, Sir, we have our own
petitioners to call before Your court.
There's Florence, caked with mud above her knees;
how long can Venice stand the lickerish sea's
unbridled fingers plucking at her skirts?
Is the next earthquake San Francisco's fault?

RAINIER

one day in seven, roughly, pokes its head
out of wool-gathering, and hogs the sky,
imposing, in the distance, on the eye.
Lo, the poor Indian looked on it as God.

Then duty-bound, correct Vancouver came
and, seeing that it never was divine,
took from a mate its new official name.
I like to see it loom from time to time:
it's picturesque — sometimes, almost, sublime.

MR. MOLE ADMITS IMPEDIMENT

Precisely what he had in mind she said
or hummed out loud
the tune that he'd been brewing in his head

and he'd have rendered: she need not have borrowed!
He knew propinquity
of the blind, burrowed flesh, but he was cowed

by this assumption: she took a liberty
in saying *Snap!*
She read his look, disturbed, spelt out that she

could feel herself at fault for some mishap....
A root of suffering's in telepathy.
Together they were pinned: she'd sprung the trap.

It clicked upon him like a thunderclap.

INCOMPATIBLES

Somewhere a door slams, and it will again:
I lie on edge, in wait,
And wince before the crash. I strain

My ears against a hum of dust, translate
Each chance remark
That tells of grudging wood, and the wind's ache.

My eyes brim dizzy in the teeming dark;
I have to sham
Dead to the world. Could I but strike a spark

Or breathe a word to tell her where I am!
I cannot rise
But hear an exit line in every slam,

Slam, slam the whopping door supplies —
This has gone on all night. In vain
I long to warm her feet, kiss dry her eyes....

Somewhere outside I hear her as she cries
Against a door that slams, and will again.

PENDANT

The frail thread snaps: pearls scatter.
Hardly a cascade,
and yet the few poor brilliants made
terrible clatter.

And some, still skirling, roll
to deeper hideaways.
Still there are days
when one more bowls

me over, squeaky
beneath my tread;
winks as I make my bed,
knowingly, cheeky.

You say you want no share
in spurious keepsakes, paste:
well, you have taste.
Not all that's rare

is precious. See:
out of a partial light
how dull they are, how slight —
stage jewellery

for a stupid play
that flopped.
Now that the curtain's dropped
for good, I'll cast away

every tricky gem
I took for legal tender.
O, who will render
me free of them?

Glints of memory
still play upon my breast,
where, once or twice, you pressed
radiant, attached to me.

DIVORCING

Lust puffs her face: her sweet breath croons.
Faint music strains from the next room.
The window implicates a moon
Chipped by the shifty fret of leaves.

A silk thing slithers from a chair.
Her thighs with mine combine, and there
Is some commingling of hair:
Her husband's in Los Angeles.

And two breasts set themselves apart
Like those I thought I knew by heart,
My hand is not much moved to chart
The salient alterations.

Brisk clockwork keeps each tick distinct,
Reminds us, crisply, that we think —
Eyes staring upward, hands unlinked —
In terms of separation.

A moth's soft kite clamps to the ceiling:
A curious face there — plaster peeling —
Twists to a parody of feeling
True love, or least resistance.

There is a warping sense of how
Unspeakable questions plague her brow
Senselessly. This will do for now.
Let all this keep this distance.

SANSON

Father to son, and son again; our skill
Is sovereign to the State, and surgical.
Crimes breed like maggots, and her body sweats
With disaffection: bad blood must be let.
Your common hangman is a bloated leech,
A more instinctive guzzler, but I teach
My axe the scalpel's business, trim my whip
To pinch the poison out of limbs, or lips.
Treason, sedition run like pus: I lance
The filthy scabs and garboils of sick France.

The fever mounts, as France falls to her knees
And ratches up her lingering disease;
I make no diagnosis, but perform
The proper cautery: sickness has many forms.
They say the land is rotten at the core,
A cancerous crown, the court a running sore
Chafed by its follies — they shall laugh no more:
My lords must curtsey to a raw-boned queen
And I, her consort: *vive la guillotine!*
Successive factions sicken in their place,
And the knife shuttles at a quickening pace.
I wear no favors, serve all men alike,
And I sleep soundest in the land tonight.

And, waking, smile. You fools who catterwaul
And snigger as I rule your carnival:
You shrink if I come close, but I can go
Serene among you, know what you dimly know:
That upon me depends your standing joke.
No Crown, no church? *I* am both King and Pope.
You mayfly men, who take turns to command,
Then come to me to purify the land,
Your blood swills easy from a practiced hand.
Mine is the House that will not be deposed,
And mine the only gentle blood, that flows
Demurely in my veins, and fears no taint
Of mingling with the common coats of paint

That daily daub my altar, and my throne.
Who signs the warrant that will be his own?
I mark him mine, and quickly he appears
To pay the full obeisance of his fear
To me, to me! I only scorn the plague
That blanches all men's faces, runs its rage
Through all Estates, through court and bishopric....
I only will survive. Who dares say I am sick?

Neighbors

CARL ERNST

Carl is a big man. With flat blue eyes,
a bulbous belly, frayed suspenders, thighs
like bolsters. He has a wife,
shrewish and small. And one grown daughter, who
takes after him. Fat thighs, eyes flat and blue.

Carl works, likes television, worships force,
permits one brand of beer, prohibits coarse
expressions in his house. He owns two guns,
and his own home; thus, he has certain rights
to honor. Looters he would shoot at sight.

Law has no right to arrogate control
away from him. He grips the blackened bowl
and jabs the pipe-stem to enforce his points.
Respect his property. Define "a mob."
The first man through his gate drops like a dog.

His wife's eyes snap a picture she approves;
his shapeless daughter irons, her face unmoved.
He squints out through a window, aiming at
rickety nights of screeching tires, and shouts
as yet too distant clearly to make out.

Carl sizes up Carl's dark reflection, framed
in the black deathless pool of windowpane.
His wife turns up the television, draws
the blinds, for privacy, or lest Carl dwell
too long on darkness like a wishing-well.

DONNA JAMES

When Donna James was seventeen,
And prettier than now, she dated
A boy her age, shy, amorous,
And ordinary. So, she miscalculated.

She went with Len a month or so,
And let Len drop. And Len became
In three-four years the Lenny Joe
Of stage, screen, and recording fame.

While Donna, straight from high school, wed
Jim James, whom she believed would go
Far. Well, Jim has not done bad:
Made foreman three-four years ago.

They have a cat a kid a car
And color television: when
Jim's home at six, that turns them on
And makes their night, till half-past ten,

With prime time close-up Lenny Joe
Complete with grin, guitar, and girls...
And sponsors who tell Donna how
To junk her curlers, still have curls,

And, with a supermagic bra/
tampon/cola/facial cream,
To make the unjust years roll back, and be
Incorrigibly, seventeen.

FRANK MOSER

Frank has gone underground. Who'll tend
The square of grass Frank kept down to the end?
A squinting, humble man, whose wife was dead
And buried — a real shrew, they said.
He kept indoors all winter; when the trees
Presumed again, you'd see Frank, on his knees,
With head bent low, inquiring of the earth
What had transpired against a plot of turf
Which soon resumed its lustre. What a lawn!
One slab of emerald, and combed, and shorn —
Gum-wrappers Frank would pocket, and stray leaves,
And trespassers spray dead: still, he'd retrieve,
Humbly, some brash kid's ball, and stand, and grieve....

Now Frank's gone underground. "He wasn't proud,"
The neighbors all agreed — at least, allowed.
A little, puzzling man, much like a mole:
You'd say he loved that lawn with all his soul
To see him mow it, wield the careful shears,
And, hatless, blinking — sweat can look like tears —
Watch his new sprinkler raise its wheeling veil,
Fan in the sunlight like a peacock's tail,
All day lay down its soft incessant flail.

BETTY LUSTY

Betty Lusty's on her way —
just the same as yesterday,
slams the car door, pulls away
with a lurch.

Betty Lusty wears hot lips,
black net stockings, heels that trip,
skirts garnished with a flounce of slip
trailing.

Betty Lusty's rouge and lace
do not charm her into grace,
redeem a flat cosmetic face:
she's homely.

Betty Lusty is a laugh.
We say, half-jokingly, and half
something else: "There's Betty off,
again."

Grandfather knew of scarlet women,
Mother would have thought her common,
now we say she's only human:
poor dear Betty!

Where she ventures no-one knows,
nor claims to care, but we suppose
anything we fancy goes
with Betty.

One short suburban block supplies
every old name of quality:
anger, sloth, and avarice
peek through curtains,

and gluttony has learned to slim;
envy and pride are in the swim,
ask all their valued relatives in,
and watch for Betty Lusty.

REX SLATTERY

Through a fine sieve
his sight's trained;
scans over faces
as if snow-blind.
Sparse, ice-blond

hair peaks his brow.
He keeps aloof.
Contempt for these surroundings
Can force his laugh,
a cougar's cough.

If he speaks, plants
words like pitons.
Chimneyless, quick
to clash together curtains,
his house is spartan.

The town holds nothing
to discover.
His ways and means
rope tight together:
no wife, no lover.

Weekends are footholds in
a life of crevices.
Then, he scales above us,
has mountains for mistresses,
friends in high places.

HELEN McBRIDE

Beautiful eyes, in a face turned forty,
yammer for help, for release from the duty
of looking their best till they drive themselves dotty.

Once she roused men as dull as potatoes,
made their eyes bulge: now those good looks turn traitor,
with merely a rooted regard they treat her.

Because his glance showed him at one with her mirror,
she tore at the face of an old admirer:
a cheat and a cheapskate she called him, an error

she was partly glad he found hard to forgive her.
Twenty years back, they had planned their world over.
How could she suffer so seasoned a lover?

Beautiful eyes: all injustices hurt them.
They stand wide with dismay at the patent corruption,
the falling-away that obtains all about them.

PATROLMAN ERICKSEN

He held a buckled hubcap in one hand
and measured skidmarks with an easy eye.
Once he began an undistinguished hum
then checked himself, but seemed indifferent why
a bunch of kids with little else to do
should drive and drink and drink and drive and die.

His name was pinned not too close to the heart,
a pistol hung demurely at his thigh,
the radio chirked and chattered in his car
which winked an unaffected bright blue eye.
He counted bodies off. It was his job
to look and see and judge and write no lie.

He'd say he had no time for poetry.

MIKE YARMOLINSKY

Big, blond, and happy, he looks good
even in confinement,
and innocent of a single glance
at this week's assignment.

What should he care if Anna kills
herself, if Levin marries,
who rushed more than two hundred yards
in thirty-seven carries,

scoring three times? The orthodox
pronounce his All-American name.
I put a case for patronyms:
he thinks I play the weirdest game.

Books dwindle in his huge red hands....
O holy Russia, sacred cow,
your herds and their great teacher are
fully translated here. I plough

such alien furrows that Mike wears
the same (in my conceit) bemused,
sweet, patronizing smile that watched
that mad Count Tolstoy hammer shoes.

A CHANGE OF MOOD
for Ran Hennes

On Second, at Main,
Homesickness calls me. Nothing I could name
Induces it, nothing in sight
Affords me correspondence; even the light
Is clearer, sharper here — yet, all the same,
I feel I might
Be standing where the High Street drifts into Church Lane.

A whisper in my ear — how plangently
It echoes — summons me back,
Proposes to my eyes
How the rank ivy pries
Along the churchyard wall, whose dry
Sandstone peppers the air, and how the black
Frets of the yew-tree pink the evening sky,

And clogs my throat with treacly mustiness
Brewed in the village sweetshop's huge glass-stoppered jars....
The humbug of nostalgia!
A police car's
Outrageous hee-haw dins
A block away, displaces my distress
With a live prickling along my skin —
Smalltown, America, swarms right back in

On that insistent note, proclaims
Its vital difference. Nothing to do with names,
Nor sights, smells, even taste; but tone of voice....
Lights switch, and I am shooed
Across, no choice,
From sunned to shady sidewalk, set aflame
By vivid accent, the imperative mood

Of PARK. EAT. DONT WALK. As who might say
Get Rich, Get Smart, Get lucky — or Drop Dead.
Live in the present all the signs convey,
And that invigorates; or stuns.
Where I was bred,
A mild persistence never pressed its claim.
My knife-edge blunted as I scraped away
Moss from the gravestones' perishable names

To help a tourist — some American chap
Hunting forefathers two centuries back.
Later, I walked him down the High Street. Faded blinds
Whispered through dust: *Gents Outfitter & Hatter,*
Antiques, Old-Fashioned Teas. A cross, and plaque,
Recalled *Our Glorious Dead.* And down the wind
The chiming hour spoke softly': "Never mind."
And "No-one's fault." And "In time, nothing matters."

LONDON AIRPORT

How the first shudder and dip
As we veer towards landing
Shatters our pressurized fellow-feeling!

We are all brought down to earth. But for these —
Suddenly — alien folk it is nothing more
Than a jumping-off place, a foot in the antique door

Into Europe. My tread is more wary. Alone,
Stepping into conventional English air,
I feel my skin tighten, and my nostrils flare.

Say the animals served just a term in the zoo,
Which then turned them loose, back where they came from,
Would they not come home

Something like me? — although I
Have enough human pride
Not to be seen trigger-kneed, bug-eyed,

And enjoy few illusions of freedom. But if they
Felt something like joy, so do I. And a new sense of danger,
And the pangs of a hunger

Which may not be satisfied, ever.
Though I smile at the guy
With a camera looped round his neck, wave goodbye

To the girl I sat next to, I'm less civilized
Than they might imagine. Though London has no Central
                                                          Park,
And less simple violence, it too can stand for the dark

Bristling, veined with essential intimations
Of terror and love, rank with remembered scents
That teach me how I am haunted, how I must hunt.

CALLING BACK

Was child:
would shy from mirrors,
hide from visitors,
cry nights, ghosts
hear squall.
Shrank close, stared small
at black wax tulip thrust-
ing from blank wall,
or cobra hood that whirred,
unstirringly,
high harsh catarrhal call

Mother. Hospital.

Watched woman rise, walk, grasp,
yank from cradle:
speak brisk, gasp,
let fall:
run into garden, calling…
(Life long, he will recall
how heart turned oracle,
coils swing, twist tense, recoil.)
Hand moved, heart stalled.
Mouth to its mouth, he gave it breath,
and heard
one breathing, far away,
then words:
accents of love, and notice of a death.

ABOVE IT ALL

I stand at her highest window:
Through the burning glass,
London spreads herself for me
As if I owned the place.

She rears up her landmarks to ogle
My glance, attain my nod:
I pinpoint Cleopatra's Needle;
Could spit on Nelson's head.

From this point of vantage
I might be Sherlock Holmes
Probing her devious workings:
It's just like at the films

That let me tell Americans
"Well goodness, Belgrave Square...."
In the tone, falsely familiar,
Of "sure, I've slept with her...."

In a different movie
There's a sloppy, dumb
Fellow who lusts for glory,
And runs away from home.

At first he does quite nicely:
One night he billets where
The wife he left behind him
Is the house's top-notch whore.

Such things can happen,
And dislocate a man.
I and my belonging
Might well be on the moon

That, yet to vanish, thinly
Blemishes the air.
Such a diminished presence
Has little business here.

Once — even at the level
Of the street that teems
With dwindled life beneath me —
I lived here. Now, the Thames,

Heavy with litter, crinkled,
Captures my eye, the pin
That shivers on the wrinkling of the water,
And does not prick its skin.

REVIEWING THE MALVERNS

Here I was childish: this the view I commanded.
Now all the faces are altered: some have unfairly
withdrawn themselves from the sight
of featureless hills, embossed
on the skyline just as I left them;
just as the mind's eye promised,
their long parade.
                     But they are dead set
against realignments: now they tell me
they do not take order from me, they are not disposed
to welcome me back, never shared any weakness
for me with those so quickly gone under the weather
that the hills ride out in their old formation,
locked into step like the years,
and the churchyard's rank and file.

BOXING DAY

As far as I hark back, a slide of hours
down the mild day, bland the air;
winter suspended, but no breath of spring,
perpetual solstice, equanimity.
Some bird called sparingly, the cool
buttermilk sunlight, chapel of slow clouds
fanned a thin flit of shadows, and like mould
the dark at length spread up from the dark earth
to brim the windows, point reflections there
of plundered tree, crazed foil, frayed tinsel, trains
derailed, the moderate hopes fulfilled,
the tedious satisfactions; time for bed.
Why should this be what I have wrapped up best —
blue of that heaven softly venomous —
as if to use again, from my first childhood?

A STALL AT SALISBURY

Stone struts, and pinnacles mount up
to stress a crucial point to which I tend:
when the eye leaps, depend
on it, the mind takes wing, pursues
one line of argument beyond the blue
fabric of limits, till the props
of reason buckle, drop away,
and faith alone
directs its craft, fulfils
the earliest promise, bringing home
to every prodigal, where he still may
find welcome, if he will.

George Herbert's view, across the dewy meadows,
small works, and railway station,
still sees the steeple lance
for heaven, still advance
its pointed indication.
Here, in this close, and later, a thin shadow
marks time, slanting across
the neat square of shorn grass,
tapers to nothingness. Come night,
sitting in darkness, it suspends
a glowing stub to warn all flights
of what they hazard, whereabouts it ends.

Seen clear from Bemerton, that pilot flame
quickening in the gloom
is love made evident:
its gleam of crimson claims
one drop of Christ's blood in the firmament,
renders the streams
fresh with salvation. Is my waste ground
parched beyond thirst; will my cold stone
be yet wrought to aspire?
O I'll leap up to my God, who pulls me down?
Voices of workmen banter through the choir,
restoring masonry, they drown

the luring echoes. Down the aisle,
(methought I heard one calling, *Child*)
out into daylight, squinting up, I stroll,
gaping at grace, and roll
wide eyes to marvel at the finger aiming
its slim hope at the air.
I send the gaze of admiration climbing
to falter where
stone issues its directive. Higher yet, there shines
a jet that, faithfully
scrawling a hazy index to the times,
zips up the sky.

CATHEDRAL CLOSE

An hour or so past noon — on winter days
So bland it seems no season, or as if
The solstice holds for ever, air all still —
The steeple's fine-spun shade minutely shifts
Onto, across those buckled roofs, and pays
Its due patronal call on each white sill.

Subject to hourly mood, it stabs or palls:
Etches a bladed outline on the snow,
Midsummer, cuts a stark deliberate swathe
Aslant the vibrant lawn, the dazzled walls;
Cuts short its midday rounds, and may forgo
All visits should the weather misbehave.

The tenants here still take their time by clocks —
Deep-bellied resonant monsters as a rule —
Which clank out quarters, drop gruff hints at night,
And count the children off to bed or school.
Yet, by this sundials' orbit, we invite
The watchman's gospel of that pointed *vox*

humana which the spire lays down
With measured weight, but no frenetic creed:
A comfortable voice, whose echoes round
Off all disputes, all heresies amend;
Decent, and kind: although not all we need
Enough for a beginning, or an end.

ANTHROPOLOGICAL

There are these people who relished their dream of the Dragon,
chanted eloquent prayers and cast spells, till the dragon came,
gobbled the ones marked out as prime dragon-fodder,
and fell fast asleep. There he lay:
they had realized their dream so entirely,
they hung by the threads they wove for a dragon to dream.

There was no escape: every route was blocked by the dragon's
slumberous bulk. There were those who wished him away,
chanted eloquent prayers, cast spells for dissolution.
But the fact of him loomed up so large that the simple notion
there might be no dragon was clearly a hopeless delusion —
no dragons in fairy tales: children had dragonless dreams.

Which meant, of course, that everyone slept that much sounder,
and awoke to the fact that the dragon's standard of sleeping
determined their habit of life. It was surely better:
no more loud quarrels, for fear of rousing the dragon;
lest the dragon lose sleep, they conversed in more musical accents;
the dragon served well as a rallying-point of consensus;
they quieted their brats with threats they would waken the dragon.

All this was a good time ago. The dragon still sprawls there.
In his shadow, under the hang of rigorous wings,
is shelter: crops fertilized with his excretions
do well. An atmosphere tinged with sulphur
is the natural air they breathe. They almost embrace the error
of thinking him dead, till his breathing judders and fumes,
as he shifts in his sleep, with a scaly clatter,
or an eyelid totters, a blink of the furnace,
a hellish wink mocking their vision. They blench
when a hot stench blasts them: though they have lost faith
in the ancient spells, and the sonorous chants, they gibber
meaningless things, clawing to cling together
in their sultry night, at the growl of a terminal thunder.

THE LION'S SHARE

The bars, being there, slice lions down to size:
this one was mighty brave to take the air
of wintry London; glum, he stood
regardant on his skimpy field of mud,
and suffered our clear stare
with a prim wincing of uncivil eyes.

We looked around him, smug, and almost bored
by weight of haunch and shoulder, lean
intake of loin, the paws' disarming pudge.
His jaw's hard slant, the bitter lemon wedge
of face seemed merely mean,
seedy, familiar. Till he roared.

Not in grand rage, not raw magniloquence
of appetite; more in the passive voice
of utter boredom: *God, I've been mucked enough,*
said his large grumble as the grudging cough
lurched out of him. And blew the bars
apart, that instant, screamed our common sense

of hearing, in recoil. Not mere loud sound,
the living voice is fleshing-out of breath.
We felt his press on us, the crisp of hair
scorched by his rancor sulphuring the air —
no breathing-space with death
one leap away — and then our weak eyes found
(the bars being there) they were just looking round.

OVERTURE: 1832

(Much detail here is drawn from Chapter 6 of L. T. C. Rolt's
Isambard Kingdom Brunel.*)*

Hayfields and gravelpits in Kensington:
the cultured musk twines scent with good cigars
in the walled garden, on midsummer nights
when Felix Mendelssohn
charms the piano in their drawing room
to sketch the harmony of stars,
till, at an upper window, Mamma sets
the tactful beam of her domestic moon
to steer the girls to bed, the young men home.

Consider Fanny as she takes her diary
into her smiling confidence: these gentlemen
with their romantic names!
As yet not even joking dreams of Mary
yielding to Isambard: how could one then
smell, on the still air, more than the stale combustion
of neighbors' hayricks? Times
are not yet prime for smog, urban congestion,
or Church Street winding down to Ponting's, Derry & Tom's

glutted with merchandise from every land
still unsurveyed, ungridded as she scrawls
her doubts of Mr. Brunel's sense of humor.
His brisk footfall
picks out the beat of railroads planned as grand concerti,
sempre accelerando. High above the city,
night's brilliant rivetting: he hears
the world tune up, pitch to that higher key
where he would tap the music of the spheres.

THE ANIMAL-LOVER

Good dog, Argos,
bedded in the shit,
good dog, easy:
can you hear him yet?

Up the beach he crunches,
relishing each stone;
seaworn nostrils pinching
the special salt of home.

Lie quiet, Argos —
running sores and fleas —
dying to infect him,
hatefully diseased.

He wants no commotion:
he's had enough of fighting.
His wife's as chaste as ever:
he might just invite them

to stay a little longer
till they've heard all his tales.
Really, all he wants to do is
flop down like a sail.

Good dog, Argos,
rag and bone and mud.
Good dog, greet him,
change his mind to blood.

When you growled to see them
make themselves at home,
did they try to win
you over with fat bones,

until they came to call you
damned thankless sneaking cur?
Did you choose neglect
eking out the years

until the moment — now —
when he passes by?
Lay back your ears,
judder your rump: his eye

flickers — my dog! Argos!
jerk your rusty tail,
let your last gasp trigger
his colossal kill.

Lie quiet, Argos:
although, at his side,
you may jog no longer,
he will stand supplied

with your old companions:
the bow, the bristling sheaf
of arrows, like a mouthful
of unfailing teeth.

He will draw the bowstring
taut, and deftly —
good dog, Argos —
unleash it, swiftly.

THE BATTLE OF BRITAIN

These beaches are not littered
with unexploded shells;
nothing here to tell
of strife, except a shattered
pillbox, the Martello

tower sunk on the Crumbles.
Vacant, the blue sky overhead,
and trim new roofs the only red
in sight. No cannon mumbles
across the map of meadows

where troops of lumpish cattle
fan to deploy their mood
of conscientious lassitude.
The only smoke of Battle
puffs from Beacon Vista's pseudo-

Tudor chimney-pots. All clear,
far as one sees, the basking hills
return their casualties as nil:
there's no contest here.
On one side, stunted willows

march as a crookleg river winds,
and, here and there, some mildly flustered
crophead greensmocked rustics muster
and straggle into lines
or huddled ambuscadoes —

cut off, demoralized, unmanned.
Through their tattered scrim,
rakish, clean-limbed
pylons strut across the land
with arms akimbo.

SCANT JUSTICE

The General's high-octane breath,
his great grey sigh of a car,
a ghost sweating out his *Memoirs* —
all of these are

luxuries to Maud,
who has a WELCOME mat,
the silver spoon that Nanny left her,
photos of her cat —

luxuries to Bogger,
who has the wind up his sleeve,
the *Financial Times*, a bench by the river,
iced air to breathe —

luxuries to Stavros,
who has lice, weak knees,
a light in the eyes, diminished sexual prospects,
and a lucky bootlace. These

spell luxury, now, to the General:
stern black headlines warn
Maud of a blow to Moderate interests,
and help keep Bogger warm.

THE HORROR MOVIES
for Richard Lindley

*"Some Jews, under menace, become Nazi thugs, learn to strut in
uniform and beat their fellows. Children sit huddled on the public
streets, stick-limbed, dying, their eyes huge and confused. And
someone trained a lens on them: always one comes back to that."*
– from a review by John Coleman of the film *Requiem for
500,000*, assembled by Jerzy Bossak and Waclaw Kazmierczak
from material shot by cameramen of the Wehrmacht, SS, and
Gestapo: *New Statesman*, 25 December 1964.

I fear this instrument
Of moral anaesthetic:
One moistureless dark eye,
Transfixing the event,
Its fixative applies:
An inhumane aesthetic.

The filming coldness seeps
Back to the eye, the hand
That regulates, depresses —
What else is it possesses
The man to squint, adjust his stand,
When he might turn away and weep?

— To see a boy burst into fire,
Ricepaper skin peel off in strips;
A woman carefully inspects
The crawling sky: the lens admires
Her child, asprawl, and on whose lips
A beady fly prospects.

And you, whose bland well-nurtured rumps
Plump out your plushy seats:
Disregard perspective,
Don't tell me of technique.
The cutting is effective?
The pans are running jumps

At what men have to live for
If we are not to freeze
Into cool, observant
Precision instruments
Of Art for Art's sake, please...
O Jesus, what I'd give for

Some straying out of focus,
Some small home-movie goof;
Better, the fine edge of strain
Lacing precision: proof
That what whirs like a locust
Is not man, but machine.

Or just an artless lecture
Furious enough for art:
Look here, upon this picture,
And turn and look on these,
The view of *War's Disasters*
That devastates the heart.

Francisco Goya fecit —
The formal phrase confines
The passion gone to make it,
The discipline that kept
Blood from slubbering the lines
His raging pencil mapped.

On each, the mind that mocked at,
Cursed, tasted what it drew,
Speaks out: the titles cryptic:
These too. So much and more.
The words are plain and few:
This is not to be looked at
Is hard by *This I saw.*

VENICE AND THE LOOKING-GLASS

In Venice, in a window, in a mirror —
a lucid stretch of light pooled by its frame
of bosky cherubs plumping for enjoyment —
she caught herself, already caught there. Not
self-seeking, knowingly: it was a shock
to meet herself, at ease, in such a setting.

Hello! she thought, *have you been here for long.?*
I hadn't realized we'd been separated.
Where did you get to?   It's so easy
to lose oneself completely in this city....
She beamed, and she was beamed on. Suddenly,
she liked the way she looked; she felt she fitted.

And walking, happy, with herself again,
it took no time at all to get quite lost
once more, in Venice, which makes ample room
for absences, reunions, subtle flittings,
the pulse and dance of highlights which its waters
glance up to illustrate a wealth of bridges.

She might have cooed: *I lost my heart to Venice....*
had Venice not restored it, in that moment
when she saw someone in the glass she favored.
No crawler, dying to be wise or witty —
herself, and stepping lively, and content to
grin like a dog and run about that city.

MRS. SCHMIDT TALKS ABOUT POLLUTION

You couldn't ever hang the wash outside:
The wind would blow our way. My Heinrich's cuffs,
All nice and white, got blackened with the stuff
Before he'd been an hour at work. We tried
To keep things decent, always took a pride
In our appearances, but just a puff
Of air would make us smutty. Like black fluff,
But sort of greasy, too: it never dried
But smeared our hands — the devil to get clean.
And this new soap we tried just made things worse.
Gritty, it was, and never lathered rightly.
Funny to think of now, of course: it's been
So long since then, but oh dear, what a curse —
Living near Dachau, back in forty-three.

FREEZING LEVEL

Outside, the snow has stopped: the final few
fritillaries have wavered down, and now
the stars confirm a quiet and compound freezing.
The world's turned scholarly,
its dirty habits not to be supposed
for the duration.
Only the distantly demented wheezing
of some fool's car that's dying on the hill
sustains a vulgar sense of civilization.

Indoors, the music glints: the lovely light
artillery of Mozart concentrates
our fire's loose structures into dazzling
salons and galleries
which blaze and buckle, yet remain composed
for the duration.
Only your scent, silk's rustle, sudden bristling
of skin that grazes skin make me recall
a lucid précis lives in limitation:
we lose ourselves in placid meditation.

Next morning's thaw returns the roads to slush,
buttery sunlight, bitter tangs of ash,
fat milksop clouds across the scoured sky dawdling,
life's charge and battery
renewed. Once more, the world's disposed,
for its duration,
to muck and muddle. The radio bubbles maudlin
lovers' farewells. And we're not in the mood
for crystal or cadenzas, constellations

nailed down by order. Strain to inflict
slavery on the stars, but blink, and space is flecked
with random sparks again. We seek control in
gracious forms, but more such silvery
harmonic nights could freeze our hearts, impose
on them mere fabrications.
Welcome again, dreck, flotsam, junkyard, sprawling
limbs of life, of love, of steaming trees
nodding their heads,
shedding the weight of brilliant condensation.

MISTRAL
for Donald Davie

"The poet falls to special pleading, chilled
To find in Art no fellow but the wind."
– Davie: *The Wind at Penistone*

Provence equates
Her poet with a wind, which frets
The trees lop-sided, cultivates
The peasants' rancor, sets
Their nerves, and teeth, on edge.

This sounds more like the truth
Than talk of potent form, a popular voice
Which "legislates,"
But leaves one little choice
(Beyond sour grapes)

Except to live, man among men,
And only whet one's tongue to praise
The generous spirit's evidence
Of love for anything well made
And making sense.

And, when one comes to speak, to fan
One's words into a local breeze
So mastered, figured, and refined
It stirs the very few, who mind
Not what it does, but is.

FIRST OF THE NINTH

and it came to an end. Someone plucked
at his sleeve, and pointed. He looked round
and saw them all clapping.
The clowns!
All squeezing invisible concertinas,
the mime so absurd the sense of such wheezing
made his eyes buzz. All out of time:
black elbow-vents
flapped in the breeze, shot rippling dents
through stiff shirt-fronts. Black velvet breasts
rhythmically pressed
and cleaving asunder; some smacked a hand
down into the other, some hit up from under,
some patted butter.
Look at that girl with her arms in a stutter,
and her sister trying to trap a
moth in her gloves; their mother
over and over at prayer. So many pairs
of pincers and clappers
and still going on! See that dapper
young fellow wincingly tapping
his palms into shape, and his neighbor, slapping
his almost to pulp, and that one persisting
in sketching the bulk of the fish he just missed! In-
sane! It should make him madly
incensed with such asses, if he didn't feel, oddly,
hand-in-hand with the crowd...

And at last, as (in quite
the right style) he bowed,
he could hear himself starting to smile.

THE SIRENS

Odysseus had the blarney, little more;
(He'd been at sea since he was young)
His crew had dwindled, now only three or four
Were still bound by his tongue.

A fertile coast to port — and there they were,
Wading in cash up to their knees;
Waving fat contracts, letting down their hair;
Posturing in their lingerie,

And singing all the time: of fast new cars,
Expense accounts, and service flats;
Catching the waiter's eye, exclusive bars,
Ways of evading tax.

He slammed the hatches: luckily half-deaf,
Lashed himself to the mast.
To drown their song, roared himself out of breath
With boasts of 'standing fast',

And so got by; and finally touched down
To find his premises abused
By quacks: his wife, in her hand-woven gown,
About to be seduced.

He chased those salesmen out, and put his house
In order to the last tall storey.
They set themselves, then, sire and spouse,
To win back ancient glory.

She at her loom, he with his lute —
And yet, at nights, his honest sleep
Was vexed: the blonde one, in the black swim-suit —
Would she cost much to keep?

Ah well: perhaps he *was* too old;
Besides, heir to so many kings…
His children might, in time, be told
How to come by such things

And so provide for his old age:
A long luxurious pleasure-cruise…
Odysseus turned to a blank page
And called out on his Muse.

MORAL CONCLUSIONS

As he laye unravelling in the agonie of death, the Standers-by could
hear him say softly, "I have seen the Glories of the world."
– Aubrey's Brief Lives: Isaac Barrow.

I work at endings to make endings work:
Poems that finish with "a click
like a box closing" is the trick I seek.

A life should end as well. I keep a store
of grand finales: Raleigh's, or Voltaire
lighting on words to cap the striking hour

with one last stroke of wit. Was it just luck
that prompted him to an immortal joke?
Or could it be a lifetime of technique

renders one prone to happy accident?
Can we maintain a discipline that won't
let us conclude in chaos, or in cant?

May we assume a habit of good talk
won't let us die of *grand mal d'esthétique?*
Brave words, where are you when the voice must break?

Will you stand by us at the last, demanding
that our last pinch of mortal understanding
should rouse our speech to make a decent ending?

I grant you that this tone's unsympathetic:
a rigid form, no welter of exotic
images, questions that prove didactic

are none of them in fashion. Nor is saying
that fashion takes short views, and shies from seeing
the Glories of the world. Neither is dying:

unravelling in agonie. The man is sick?
No pun in Aubrey's title? Mere rhetoric?
Thank God for anaesthesia? Heretic,

if I were reading this to you, aloud,
you might be sure I schemed it to provide
a good ill-favored moral to conclude

the evening's entertainment. Look,
we've travelled no great distance by the clock
towards the final box's formal click,

putting full-stop to all we choose to speak.

THE CHECK-UP

Submissive to the doctor's will
I lay my watch down on the window-sill
And poke a limp hand forward. Time stands still

And holds my breath up as his fingers clutch;
Credulous, huddled in its shaky hutch,
Heart flinches from the cold professional touch —

Dud? Dud?
— And then the ignorant swagger of my blood
Perks up against his thumb; that liquid thud

Is regular as clockwork, lets me be
Myself again. "Good for a lifetime," he
Concludes; that tone of comic sympathy

Is made to measure; yes, he has the trick.
He turns to wash his hands. Well, that was quick.
And on my wrist again the tick tick tick.

DANDELIONS

Migrants, they prosper anywhere
there's scope for their light industry's
cheap goods, random expansion.
Fool's gold cogs the grass:
drab leaves, fat sappy stems cast up
wheels packed with garish flanges,
false teeth for fake lions, glaring,
soon dull in jamjars.

Last night, though, moonlight furred
their muted, ghostly aspect:
lawns mealed with mothball skulls,
pocked, soft to the finger.
To-day, children consult them,
puffing for hours, compete
to make time fly, dispatch flotillas
to form new colonies, establish foundries.

SNOW DADDY

Her snowman sports his shabbiest hat; she squeaks
piercingly as she jabs
a pipe he used to own
his favorite, roughly where the mouth would be
if he had ways to speak.
For eyes, she picks out two black shiny stones.

And now she chatters down his weak
demurs at the resemblance
that she insists on, and will dance
around the solemn buffer who conforms
to what her fancy wishes, till she must
submit to being fed, and loved, and warm

once she has changed. And then, how soon
only a greying lumpishness remains
blobbing the caustic green, and every day
shrinks more into itself, and out of sight
of her concerns. At last, the rain
has whittled all but two small stones away.

FINAL DIRECTIONS

I hate a tended grave. Save me a place
to go to seed in, growing so absorbed
some craft beyond a common practice shapes
my plot and has me, breathless, utter
what comes most natural. There's a point
where skillful trimming is the work of hacks:
death should be one word no-one can compose
neat settings for. With life ruled out at last
it's time to wax romantic, and go dead.

If there's a stone, I want that soon to sag,
lurch in the fetters ivy loops about it,
relinquish all distinction. I trust the various weather,
lichen, and snail make epitaph a cipher,
and name a blank. I hope the fat
swags of rank grass, weeds bogged in succulence
thrive on what contributions I submit
to snag and ramble: let extravagance
brag in green garbled tongues that they compound
and bring to light what I could not account for:
slips of the tongue, jetsam of dreams, stray tags
of nonsense rhymes, the potpourri of fancies
a lifetime's editing rightly rejected.

I want my bones' allotment to run mad: that small
cloudburst of wilderness tell the passer-by
no more of me than, when I came to die,
confusion was my style: I lost control.

MORE NOBLE DUST

The original codex, which according to a venerable tradition was discovered wedging a wine barrel in Verona, at the end of the thirteenth century A.D., was in a poor state. There were frequent lacunae *in the text, attributable (according to the same tradition) to the operation of the wine on the parchment. Worse than this, the codex itself disappeared again as mysteriously as it had appeared, although fortunately not before at least two copies had been taken.*
– from the introduction to *The Poems of Catullus,*
translated by Peter Whigham.

How you would smile, Catullus, at this
typical flick of your own witty insolence,
if you knew that, in time,
Time's wry sense of what's fitting would screw
up your words, in one ball,
to sphincter the asshole of an old barrel
and sop up its swills
of *vin ordinaire*, in decaying Verona,

and laugh at the scholarly pickle that issues
out of the wodge of soggy papyrus
at long last uncorked.
Deploring a codex foxed with chianti
and the flagrant bouquet
of indelicate Eros, a corps of dry cleaners
laced the lacunae
of Lesbia's panties, made shifts for graffiti,

lamented the blotches an immodest time
and wine's operation inflicted. But what
of the waste of the drink
that wasted the words, yet in turn took a tincture
of spirit from song?
Did that rough *paesano* admit a refinement,
fine palates detect
a lyrical tinge, strain of carmine in rouge?

Who stayed at the inn? Did staid Veronesi
stop for a glass, start frisking the maids?
Was the priest there unfrocked?
Did the girls snatch their skirts, did toper and tenor
vie for snatches of song
and find their tongues twisting to liquorish Latin?
And what of the lovers,
lost and belated, looking for shelter

and sober repose, who then couldn't sleep,
but frolicked the night out, shaking the bed —
partly with laughter —
at feeling their limbs pressed to sensual inventions,
matching carols of lust?
Were the artists there lively? Was life then an art
as easy as drinking?
Did their poems infuse that life they were steeped in

before the cork popped? Lees of that vintage
wrinkle the dust; to dust crinkled
the poetry — dry, you may say.
Do you really drink vinegar? Read for a stopgap?
Chew on dry corks?
How you would laugh, if you could, at Catullus,
who made only songs
good for centuries, for stopping a bung-
hole; mouthfuls of living
in a dead tongue.

SUCH SMALL DEER

Old photographs perplex:
We cannot quite conceive
Those blooming, faded children
Could pass for us, nor quite retrieve

What are, for us, still lives. I see
My namesake, with a toy
Bear nuzzling his ear: what
Secrets can they enjoy?

We work up smiles to see ourselves
Laughing, at play. But never
In kids at *Happy Families*
Quite comprehend ourselves, each other,

Or sister, perched on Brownie,
Faint ink: *May '48.*
We recognize the animal
(The girl's quite out of date)

And view, with more affection
Than for our past, the pets
Who show up here and there, and seem
Somehow, more real. And yet —

How obvious, how the obvious shocks! —
How dead they are. Old Java:
Even his great-grandkittens now
Are gathered to their fathers.

Or rather, if one trace remains
Of Ptolemy, or Tigger,
Or Tigger's kittens, one might light
Somewhere on a sliver

Of fraying bone, or even
A flat barbaric skull,
Snarling, picked clean, and packed with dirt;
Not sleek nor strokeable

But indescribably remote
From nursery illustrations
Of loving animals...I think
Of small beasts' skeletons,

The cunning of the linked and locked
Interdependence, filigree-
work of vertebrae,
Breathless fragility

— Something I first saw as a child:
The child these snapshots claim, that must
Blanch, dwindle, grow still more delicate,
Whitening into dust.

A STAGE OF DEVELOPMENT

*Matthew Henson, Commander Robert Peary's black
servant, raised the U.S. flag at the North Pole, April 1909.*

*Right on the nose of the Pole
Peary's nigger breaks out the flag.*
In the middle of nowhere someone
Shakes out a rag.

*Blotting the spotless canvas
A hooligan smudge of burnt cork.*
Against the blackboard the teacher's
Face flares out like chalk.

A chimneysweep soiling the linen.
A snowman stuck in the coal.
Turning the country upside down.
Giving the nation its soul.

Positive action, and now.
Negative: stop or we shoot.
Something is blowing in here:
It could be detergent. Or soot.

MISTER MAN

Mister! they yell, and then, still sharper, *Mister!*
and bring me down to earth. Rough grass, and mud.
What can they...? Oh. Get on the ball:
bounce, soggy bounce, hop-toad, rolls dead
a yard away. They all fall silent. Watch me.
Dunlop to take the penalty. In his best shoes?
Oh well. And oh, how well it feels:
punching it square and soundly, grooving out
a long inch-perfect cross to that fair boy
whose hands snap off his hips, who traps it cleanly,
veers, pulls all eyes his way. They might say thanks?
But *Bill!* they scream — *here, Bill! Bill, pass!* and stream
towards the distant goal. Damn it: a smear
on my new YoungLook slacks: lucky I didn't go
arse over tip. *Pass, Bill, you idiot:*
get rid of it. Ah, Bill, you held too long.
One thin voice, woeful, shrieks, *Oh, bad luck, Bill!* —
was that the one who needled, *Come ON Mister?*
I think one little prick squeaked, *Chuck it, Pop.*

WALKING THE DOG

Sick of the tetchy, intermittent scolds
my flesh and blood emits from its deep cot,
sick of the hot
preposterous impotence
that scalds my throat, but leaves her grace quite cold,
until I half-admire the fine, controlled
achievement of her flaming nonchalance —
the bitch can make a six-month-old
New Yorker yield her fresh intelligence —
sick of the lot,
I snatch, plume, whistle up
my coat, intention, almost full-grown pup.

Outside, it's dark: frost
edges the air.
I mark the sudden prick
of the dog's ears, and thrust
of his contentious muzzle, swear
correctly at him — but I nearly sic
him onto pussy where
she freezes, hunched, malevolent.
How I could envy him that quick
and finished sense
of unresolvable difference!
"Good boy," I mutter, easier on the chain:
I take back 'bitch,' again.

The farthest houses sink behind us:
I snap him free —
he lunges off, interrogates a tree,
then, in the easy, fluent, mindless
flush of his long-legged ecstasy,
sweeps round in circles of pure running,
until I catch the trick, beginning
to sprint, swerve, dodge as he comes bombing
in, like a young typhoon....
We sprawl together in the damp deep grass;
grabbing for breath and laughter, his warm tongue at my face,
I shake my heels at the moon.

OLD TOM

First — just a kit — a boot squelched him,
voided his screeching innards.
Then a charged flex had him reeling,
salted his whiskers
with a fizzy icing.

Once he was drowned
though he scrabbled his ratty scrawn
out of the rainbutt, polished it off
licking the rest of his lives into shape.
Once he was stoned

by dead-end kids ganged for a killing:
he laid down his ears and scarpered
like a wink of spit off a shovel,
and counted his breaks on the rooftop.
Next, he took poison

neat from the garbage's delicatessen:
by jerks, he coughed up a lifetime
of hairballs and rotgut gobbets.
Once a tussle of yipsnapper mongrels
had him worried to death.

Once he was hanged if the clinching crook of a tree
couldn't bear him to cling to his freezing.
And once, in a yowling rut up the alley,
sharpslashers nailed him, scraped on his throatstrings,
clipped off an ear by their scoring.

Now he considers chances,
thinning his longshot eyes, switching
a nibble of tail at the odds.
He reckons his claws in, and purrs: eight down,
the hell of a tough one to go.

A CLASSIC CASE

Be careful, rooting in the basement,
what you dislodge there. Look,
don't say *these spiders are a perfect menace,*
but mind that box of books: *Alice,*
Lear, Grimm...spines stamped with gilt will catch
the eye: they tug you back
and pin you. Ragged bindings latch
on to your hands: before you know, you're hooked.
Is it dim light down there sets you to spell
the sense out? Was it that rusted nail
that pricked out liquid beads along your arm?
What *is* that sticky stuff you can't brush free from?

Get back to business, innocent adult reading:
normal enough, as all the experts vouch.
Down at the inky bottom of the well
lies poor Brer Rabbit, on Brer Fox's couch,
crying, and pleading
(and now with no false panic in his squeal):
Doctor, do anything but that!
Don't throw me back
into that briarpatch, that knot of thorns
and love-lies-bleeding,
where everything that's wrong was born,
and goes on breeding.

SUNSTRUCK

Pinned down by sun, spread-eagled,
I watch my eyelids, veined
Like grapes, thin-skinned, and changing
Under my press, from fine
Vermilion into red arterial
Roads all running wine.

Heat holds me in a truss
That reaffirms my bones.
Around my limp fist, sand
Fashions a grainy cestus;
Open and hardened, I am honeycombed
Like pumicestone.

Drowsy, I hear the sea:
It simplifies my head
Into a dusky, brimming
Cupola of bronze.
Only my belly, like a sponge,
Gluttonous, swollen,

Knows none of this refinement,
Plumps for the cool of dark,
Moon like a slice of citron,
Owls in the myrtle-grove,
Hands' questioning, silk's sibilance,
And the long squeeze of love.

In the hot mosaic
Sun prints upon my blindness,
I figure brilliant children —
Gold skins, and eyes like sloes —
One with a net and trident,
One with a golden bow.

Translations

Giovanni Pascoli
NOVEMBRE

Such glitter in the air, so clear the sun,
You look for peach-bloom to renew the summer,
Your heart picks up the whitethorn's thin
Bitter aroma…

But the thorn's tinder now; black, brittle shoots
Scratch crazy signatures across serene
And empty sky: the ground, shocked by your foot,
Hollow, it seems.

Silence all round: but, as the wind unlimbers,
Far off, from gardens, orchards, you may hear the red
Leaves' delicate downfall. This is how summer
Feels to the dead.

Guido Gozzano
LA DIFFERENZA

My thoughts go round and round. That noisy goose
That gobbles on the towpath — does *she* think?
She seems all right! As winter twilight sinks,
She stretches out her neck, rejoicing, raucous.

She hops and cackles, dives — she's fat and juicy,
But surely doesn't take time off to think
Of Time, nor dreams we're on the brink
Of Christmas, when Cook's bright tools find uses…

O gosling, snowwhite sister, little chuck,
You teach that Death is only something guessed at;
We perish only when our thought reverts

To what you've never thought. yes, you're in luck!
It really doesn't hurt to be roasted,
But think of being roasted — that's what hurts.

Giacomo Leopardi
ALLA LUNA

O gracious moon, well I remember how,
This time last year, upon this very hill,
I came, full of my grief, to look on you again;
And how you hung there then, above that wood,
As you do now, illumining it all.
But indistinct and wavering, thanks to tears
That brimmed my eyes, clung to my lashes then,
Your countenance appeared, for my life was —
And *is*, continues the same strain — so burdensome
To me, beloved moon. And yet, there's comfort in
Such memories, and in the long account
Of my affliction. Oh, how soothingly
In youth when hope still sees so far ahead,
And memory looks back so short a distance, come
Our recollections of all things gone by —
Though they're sad still, with sadness that endures!

Henrich Heine
MEIN LIEBCHEN,
WIR SASSEN ZUSAMMEN

My darling, we floated delighted-
ly close and warm in the skiff.
The night was still, and we glided
On a widening, wavering path.

Enchanted islands, enchanting
Lay dusky against the full moon,
And the swirls of mist swam, dancing
To surging and swaying tunes.

So sweet, and still sweeter, they sounded
And surged to and fro — but we
Were bound to pass by, and found no
Solace in all the wide sea.

SQUARE

is what you may call me, and welcome.
Should I be ashamed
that the trendy patter would place me
in a pride of resonant names?
Quadrangle, cloister, piazza,
the marketplace —
wherever men like to be serious, or need to
develop a sensible space,
they tend toward squares; of all games
the purest is checkered: giving
reason to pastime, and logic its music, is,
by definition, living.

In a pure state of Nature,
Squares may not exist, but for man
to shape his life by right angles
is natural enough; he can
neither improve upon Nature, nor live by
her crazy directions. He may only create
alternatives, ordered constructions,
a pattern becoming his state.
She squiggles and doodles, At best she
describes perfect circles, like sun
that warms the carved stone, illuminates squares that attest to
the good sense of man.

Some squares are more shapely than others:
I hope to be one
that gathers the sunlight, and offers
relief from the sun.
With room for diversion, yet ever
a center of craft, and fair trade,
and even my shadier sides maintaining
a decent façade.
Let me be wrought into balance, my lines
discover perspective, amounting
to more than the sum of my parts.
Set in the middle, performing its function, a fountain.

A LITTLE EPITHALAMIUM
for Tom and Dana

Each day's a place to move in; some
with living-room too meager
or, frankly, ruinous.
Others are lighter, brighter, bigger,
and you're at large, at home
in a fine open house
friends find welcome.

May this day be one
Time's spyglass loves to dwell on,
spot where familiar treasure
once was a new belonging. Still, on
dwindling windows may the sun
spark dazzling recollection
of here-and-now; your happiness, our pleasure.

CARUSO FOR THE CHILDREN

"Listen," I tell my children, "Listen...."
but they look blank.
I cannot force my love upon them: disson-
ance comes of that.

Nor teach them how to live: breathing
remains a lonely art.
Fathers, as well as tenors, fear
strains of the unaccompanied heart.

They play with dolls, and cars,
under the aerial span
of aria, expanding: *Ah
Ia paterna mano*....Man

needs a diversity of love
to train his voice to giving
what children need to hear. At night,
to study their soft breathing,

I stand by their dark beds as rapt
as if that quiet recitative
were of my composition, shaped
by this preserving voice that gives

so prodigal, of living art,
I think they cannot choose but hear
what I might tell them, pointlessly:
how each note weights the air

as shapely as the globe of glass
blown into contour, yet
veined with the blood's warm inspiration,
heady, exsufflicate,

as round and ripe as the good fruit
on the swayed, laden boughs
of trees of expert grafting, craft
and nature married; how

still he proposes, fifty
years since his death,
this paradoxically unthrifty
controlled expenditure of breath.

Selected Sprats, Limericks Я Us, and Assorted Ghosts

Jack Sprat could eat no fat,

His wife would eat no lean.

And so between them both, you see,

They licked the platter clean.

THE BALLAD OF JACK SPRAT
AND HIS LADY

It happened about Michaelmas
In the waning of the year
That little Jack Sprat came merrily hame
From chasing o' the deer.

His lady met him at the gate.
O welcome hame, saith she.
And hae ye brought a fallow fat
Tae feast your men and me?

I havena brought a fallow fat
But a stag o seven tines
That ran upon the mountainside
Red meat for redder wines.

O shame on you, false lord, she says,
To bring red meat tae me!
Frae this nicht on, at board, in bed
O' yours, I'll niver be.

He's taken oot his wee pen-knife
And cut her girdle free
And clapped it roond her lilie-white throat
To hang her frae the tree.

Then up and spak at little foot-page.
For shame, sir knight, he cried.
Shall it be said, for sic sma cause,
So fair a lady died?

And to her then said brave Jack Sprat —
The tear stood in his ee —
There's steak for me on yonder beast
And fat eno for thee.

Lady, be mine again, he said,
And drink a stoup wi' me.
On venison we'll soon be fed
And so we'll canty be.

And you sall be my leal leman
And I your love nichtlang.
So she held out her lillie-white hand
Nae mair was said thereon.

Then they took pleasure by the pipes
Tae dance upon the brae
And when their merriment was done
They slept beyont the day.

tr*dition*l (hb)

DOMESTIC HARMONY

or, Lines written upon hearing of the singularly felicitous
prandial Arrangements of a Friend, an Artisan, who
lived in Satterthwaite, Lancashire.

John Sprat and Sarah lived alone
beside the village common.
John was a man, a carpenter,
And Sarah was a woman.

And every day John sawed with saws
To get their simple living,
While Sarah's housework showed no flaws,
Such care to't she was giving.

They had a pig, a simple beast —
'Twas slaughtered in due season;
But not at once made they a feast —
I'll tell you now the reason.

Good old John Sprat had little taste
For bacon fat at table,
While Sarah's lean must go to waste,
Try hard as she was able.

But Sarah loved the silver fat
Scorned on her husband's plate:
John longed to sit where Sarah sate,
Eat what she never ate.

At length the pair agreed to make
A pact to help each other:
Each from the other's plate would take
And thus would end the pother.

So happy John ate all the lean
While Sarah ate the fat.
No couple I have ever seen
At gayer table sate.

From simple folk we thus can learn
— And learning is our duty —
How discords can to concord turn
And make united beauty.

W*ll*am W*ordsw*rth (hb)

UNPUBLISHED STANZAS

How strangely mutable the human heart!
Whoever sings, its constancy doth praise —
That blest emotion — never to depart —
While upon the face of faces gaze!
The wellspring of our lives — and joys — and art —
Makes moments sweet — and sweeter, length of days —
Gilds marble — then one day we're out of sorts —
We stroll abroad — and find we're in the courts.

Juan in truth was faithful — to black eyes
(While that they sparkled) — and to browns and blues
(But not to stockings) and to every size —
Tall, short, or tiny — if we speak of shoes.
And when a sated hunger quenched his sighs
One way, he'd sense enough to change his views —
Enough to take the lean and leave the fat
Like that old friend of yours and mine — Jack Sprat.

Jack and his dame agreed to disagree
(Or so the story tells us) — and the moral
As drawn by W*rdsworth, is that he and she
Were wise, since what's more senseless than a quarrel
On little points, in which a victory
Brings nothing but a twig of withered laurel?
So in some unions it goes on — perfection —
Because *two* never aim in *one* direction.

Yet I'm not sure. If, in the marriage bond,
Two tastes dissimilar are yoked together —
And there's no one thing of which both are fond —
Is it surprising if one slips the tether?
Or — like my wife — the other should abscond
As if a wedding-vow were but a feather —
With credit — bairn — her settlements — and money —
That her lord ne'er gets back, however dun he?

*L*rd Byr*n (hb)*

123

WHOLLY MILLIE'S PRAYER

In a bit biggin dwelt Jack Sprat,
His guid wife, and their auld black cat
Ca'd Millie, wha had lang syne sat
Snug in the housie:
A moggie grown fu' sleek and fat
On mony a mousie.

But och! it gars my heart fu' sair
Tae tell of a' the carking care
That had o'erwhelmed this loving pair
For sic sma' cause,
And made them amaist tae despair
O' Hymen's laws!

For sonsy Jack, when he took meat,
It made him girn, it made him greet
Tae see his Jean the lean to treat
Wi' chill disgust, O!
Though she the laithsome fat could eat
Wi' fiendish gusto!

Whiles Jean looked on him wi' despite
And scorned the loon that stuffed his kyte
Wi' rusty meat, but of the white
Took not ane helping:
He'd see, if they should fa' to fight,
Wha'd catch the skelping!

Sae Millie, seeing much amiss,
The wrack of a' domestic bliss,
Ca'd Heaven to adumbrate this
Dour interlude;
And (having taken time to piss)
To G-d she mewed:

"Lord, see how a' things gang agley,
Ha'e mercy on a mog's dismay,
Thou kens we are but bruckle clay:
Dispell oor gloom,
And gi'e us humble hearts, I pray,
And platters toom.

Knap some sense in these addled heids,
Let "share alike" be baith their creeds,
Let each supply the t'ither's needs
In peace, but then
may some bit scrappies be my meed:
Amen, amen!

R*b*rt B*rns (wd)

THE BROKEN PLATTER

Summer was it, at Mellstock Fair,
When we bought that fairing?
Little thought I, then and there,
It would have such an airing.

For you would never agree
To sample a slicing
The other was hemlock to me —
It might have been icing.

And now the china is broken
Which we were cleaning
Though it was a chancy token
Of all we were meaning.

Th*mas H*rdy (hb)

"AH, ARE YOU EATING WITH MY SPOON?"

Over Yellham Bottom the wind grew to a moan;
The elms at Stepton Dolliver set up a dreary groan:
Leasome Mead was flooded; the cows at Bullham Bud
Switched their tails curmudgeonly, and chewed a bitter cud.

At Cumberly-cum-Cropton, the barton door flapped wide,
The 'lated reddleman peered in, but noone saw inside.
All that met his starting eyes and sorely halting gait,
Were two stools, brusquely overturned, and one empty pewter plate.

Some said that Jack the journeyman had sworn an oath in youth
That never on the grosser flesh would he once whet his tooth;
And others — gossips old and sere — in mutters would debate:
"Sal Sprat would sooner thirt the yowes than red meat masticate."

The vicar called the tenor-man, and he called up the bass;
The hind who blew the serpent came at his sluggish pace.
They laid the pewter plate to rest: the skirling wind grew calm,
As over that beclovered grave they played the nineteenth psalm.

Th*mas H*rdy (wd)

GIOVANNI SPRATTO

His name was Giovanni (angelice John) Spratto. Of Parma:
he loved not violets nor the White of the Ham, though born
in a city famous for both Dainties.

He studied sometime in Queens' Colledge in Cambridge: his
chamber was over the water. He blames the beer there for
what he would incontinently pisse into the river, to the great
Scandal of onlookers. "But," said he, "if the Cam be not a
Jakes, the Queens are my wh — es." His was a pretty Wit,
and (tho' a hard scholar) he had an Eye ('twas a great gog-
gling Piggeseye) for the wenches.

He married to a comely and discreet lady: I am sorry I have
not her name. But there came betweene them great
Dissention and Unkindness, which thus arose. He was dilet-
tante di prosciutto but, as I hitherto disclosed, disdained the
Fatty part thereof. But his Lady, considering altogether other-
wise, had her gusto for the Fat alone. Thus each grew into
great disgusto with the other's Appetites, and held but little
Communication for nigh on five years.

By good fortune — 'twas Anno Domini 1638, on the
forenoon of St. Swithin's day — Mistress Sprat (She had
declared, on the wedding-day, that "she would take a Sprat in
hand, but never put To(e) to it") was seized by a Notion so
ingeniose as to put one end to all their Mischance. "Jack," as
they sat to table, "there is surely an Elephant on Mistress
Bates's housetop!" "Nay," he replied "'tis too much Hoggish
Gormandising has fattened thy Wit." "Look then out of win-
dow; see if it be not so." He (tho' grumblingly) complying,
she made Revolution of their great Platter ('twas of excellent
Pewter). So he, resuming his place, most greedily consumed
that portion she had left untasted ('twas good rich meat,
from pigs of Marlborough). She, in good recompense, fell to
the Fat he would fain have left abandoned. When all was Ate
he, observing her draw near to burst her Reins with Jollity,
inquired somewhat roughly of her what the jest might be?
"None," said she, "but look'ye, how came our Platter clean?"

This tale was borne through the towne, to the delight of all. "In faith," said Master Sprat, "the neighbors could not have laught with better heart had I been horned, not cured."

He was a slender man, somewhat choleric. He was wont to cuff his sons' ears when they construed their Virgil ill, and his wife's for but slender provisions of Parmeggiano for his table. It was lately told me he is dead, but I know not when nor where.

J*hn A*br*y (wd)

WOMEN IN DEMOCRACY

A consequence of equality is that women have much less of the art of being truly feminine than we in Europe take for granted. It was in vain that I looked for those alluring charms which in a wife do so much to soothe the life and labours of the husband. The American woman knows nothing of the rue de Rivoli and all it stands for. She has no maid; circumstances force her to be self-reliant. She is not to be found in the milliner's shop but rather, with one hand, swinging an axe to fell a forest tree while with the other, so to speak, she protects her children against alligators and rattlesnakes. She is no less devoted to her husband and to her wifely duties than is a European woman, but she is his equal partner in the business of life. I saw a striking instance of this when visiting a forest farm. It must be understood that every property on the edge of the wilderness relies for meat on the pigs which have replaced the buffalo; pork in all its forms is the staple of the American table. On reaching a certain log-cabin under the trees[1] I was hospitably greeted in true democratic fashion: that is, a stretch of earthen floor, less moist than the rest (all these cabins are built on swamps) was indicated for my night's repose, and for a fee of only twenty dollars* I was invited to share the family meal. In return I was asked only for such news as I could provide of the price of molasses at New-York. At table I noticed a touching incident of democratic wifely devotion. The peasant refused to eat any of the fat meat of the pig. His wife professed to have a corresponding aversion to the lean; so between them both they entirely cleaned a whole wooden platter — of which, alas, there was but one in the cabin. I and my companion had to eat off the table-top: such is the fine simplicity of democratic manners.

*Alex*s de T*cquev*lle (Democracy in America, vol. 5). (hb)*

[1] *AT's travel note-books establish that this episode occurred in the home of John A. Sprat, justice of the peace in Tammanny County, N.Y. – Ed.*

* *This is not considered a high price in the united states, although it is half what a Parisian labourer can typically earn in an entire year. – AT.*

CANTO CXXXII

My Arthur! when the lamp burns late
And turbid fevers vex my brain,
I seem to hear thy voice again
In its clear, thrilling tones relate

Many a mystic parable,
But, most of all such teachings, that
Which treats of yeomanly Jack Sprat,
And proves my grief consolable.

The year remorseless turned its wheel:
Unnibbled, fat grew foul and green;
Unmasticated, the rare lean
Shrank to a ghastly mummy-meal…

Can such be all we know of Life?
A thousand aeons pass, and will
The lower race of lipids still
With carbohydrates be at strife?

For all my fear, I dimly trust
In some surcease of fleshly war —
Then stalwart Jack laughed loud, and swore,
And his grim sinewy arm outthrust,

Upturn the groaning board did he,
And all to indistinction cast —
My Arthur! may it be, at last,
such melange compass thee and me!

Alfr*d, L*rd T*nnys*n (wd)

LITTERY LIMRIX:

Loquitur Sgt. Bloggs, Devon Constabulary:
Mister 'Olmes, we request your profound
Attention to what 'as been found —
The spoor, so to speak,
Not of pug, nor of peke,
But of a most gigantical 'Ound!

There's a nubile young milkmaid called Tess,
Whose deep-rooted urge to say "Yes
to Life" — that's the phallic
In Angel, and Alec,
Procures her a deal of distress.

When Eliza fled over the Ice
The Bloodhounds were loosed in a trice;
And Simon Legree,
Melted not one degree,
Snarled "Freedom? It comes at a Price!"

Henchard, in drink, became wild:
He auctioned his wife and her child,
Thus incurring much pain
When Elizabeth-Jane
Wed a Scotsman, not bitter but mild.

Poor Boldwood, could not see the joke
Of Bathsheba's milit'ry bloke;
Arrayed for the bridal
He waxed homicidal,
And she ended up Mrs. Oak.

Tom Brangwen takes up with a Pole.
Her daughter has more Will than Soul.
Her child, in due course, is
Involved with some horses —
The Rainbow survives, on the whole.

He's a crafty old bugger, that Harding;
The Jupiter says he's been guarding
Pots of money, by God!
From us silly old sods —
We'll make him cough up every farding.

Emma Woodhouse quite shocks Mr. Knightley
At the picnic. He, perfectly rightly,
Utters stern admonition
Arousing contrition
For treating Miss Bates impolitely.

Though the Warden appears mild and meek, on
occasion he simply won't weaken.
Instead, he resigns,
Which is rather hard lines
On his temporal guide, the Archdeacon.

Barchester's feminine Pope
inspires the pious with hope,
but they soon come to feel
that she's set, in her zeal,
her foot on a slippery Slope.

Mr. Crosbie's professions prove hollow,
but, through all the pages that follow,
poor Johnnie Eames
can never, it seems,
seem to Lily a valid Apollo.

(wd)

(and from hb)

Young men who are rich must get wed
(Or so it is generally said)
So Darcy and Bingley
Could not go on singly:
They married the Bennetts instead.

Of the wrath of Achilles a word:
He sulked when they kidnapped his bird.
He made Priam pray
For a night and a day
Before he got Hector interred.

Miss Woodhouse, young, handsome and rich
By some was considered a bitch.
But for Pa, whom she cherished,
Her love never perished;
And her marriage knew never a hitch.

Since Man will not do as he's told
His salvation's been put upon hold.
You cannot blame God
(though he is such a sod)
For Adam was not self-controlled.

She wanted to do something great
But was dealt a low hand by her fate:
For Casaubon's key
Was rusty, you see,
To their mutual despair, need I state?

OPERATIC LIMS

The sky is relentlessly leaden.
I feel my eyes moisten and redden.
In my heart it's December . . .
Ah well, just remember
The only good kid is a dead 'un.

Sing hey! for life in an attic
Where encounters are always ecstatic,
But brief are the flings
Of delightful young things,
And the end that they come to, traumatic.

Through what's left of Nagasaki
Stumps a Loot, no longer larky.
His bride (fresh from Phoenix)
Keeps Sorrow in Kleenex
Just so long as there ain't more malarkey.

A gentleman's gentlemen, Nick,
Proves plausible, suasive, and slick
At tempting his master
To hellish disaster,
Till Love turns the ultimate trick.

Not even the eye of a mother
Can distinguish one infant from t'other,
So the wrong babe's consumed...
When the story's resumed
The Tenor's the Baritone's brother.

That amiable klutz, Nemorino,
Becomes brave on a litre of vino
Supplied by a quack;
Though he sees things go black,
The end will be happy, that we know.

Some fellows all dressed up in kilts
Express horror when poor Lucy wilts,
But she'll slice up her groom;
And midst ancestral tombs
More blood will be desperately spilt.

Amina counts too many sheep —
The result's not too likely to keep
A lover content,
But the Count's a real gent,
Proving people do walk in their sleep.

Adalgisa is younger than Norma:
Pollione inclines to the former.
But all must give way
To the priestess's sway
When she's sung by a stellar performer.

The Swiss seek a champion to quell
The Austrian tyrant from hell.
Will he have the wits,
That fellow who splits
Apples neatly in two? Who can Tell?

You need your beard trimmed in Seville?
An elopement effected with skill?
A fool-proof tax-harbor?
Just call up the barber
And tell him to send in his bill.

The man with a hump on his back
Has a gift for the cutting wisecrack;
The blood on his mind
Is the Duke's, but he finds
It's his daughter who's given the sack.

From Rome: we hear the chief fuzz
Has been stabbed (the horrible scuz)
In defence of her honor
By a famed prima donna
Who jumps to conclude — that's the buzz.

An icy princess tries to diddle
Her way out of losing at riddles;
The prince (a barnstormer)
Gets to sing *Nessun dorma* —
Poor Liu is caught in the middle.

Celebrations down by the Nile,
Are staged in spectacular style,
But the lovers are bound
To go underground
And die — though they linger awhile.

The ladies find no antidote
once they've had the Don at their throat.
But all will end well:
he's dragged down to Hell,
and the moralists stand round and gloat.

From the Don, let us turn to Otello,
A valiant but credulous fellow;
though he writhed and he winced
he remained quite convinced
that Iago was just Leporello.

(wd)

GHOSTS

(Some paired ghosts:)

I am the ghost of good Count Leo:
Feodor writes with a certain brio.

I am the ghost of the mad Feodor:
Sometimes Count Leo's a bit of a bore.

I am the ghost of Miss Jane Austen:
The note of passion so often sounds forced in.

I am the ghost of Currer Bell:
What the lady feels I simply can't tell.

I am the ghost of the voice of La Callas:
I had the forethought to act with malice.

I am the ghost of gentle Renata:
I hadn't the sauce to compete with a tartar.

I am the ghost of Phoebus Apollo:
My oracle offers good reasons to swallow.

I am the ghost of the great Dionysius:
Divine inspirations? Mine are the diciest.

(How divinely anti-Semitic!)

I am the ghost of the King of the Jews:
Me, or Barabbas? And whom do they choose?

(from A Procurator's Memoirs)

I am the ghost of Pontius Pilate:
Judah? That hellhole I spent a brief while at?

(Ghosts Ancient and Modern:)

I am the ghost of the Emperor Nero:
Lions 70, Christians, 0.

I am the ghost of Jude the Obscure:
'A zhould 'a managed a Zecond, a'm zure.

I am the ghost of Clement Atlee.
I wasn't brilliant. I said so. Flatly.

I am the ghost of Lady Chatterley:
Mrs. Oliver Mellors, latterly.

I am the ghost of the noble Othello:
You seem an honest, reliable fellow.

(Animal ghosts:)

I am the ghost of Mansfield Park's pug:
Aunt Bertram has knitted me into a rug.

I am the ghost of the fine cat Hodge; in
The good Doctor's bosom I found a safe lodgin'.

(Lord Emsworth's portly nominee triumphs once more)

I am the ghost of the Empress of Blandings,
Sprawled at ease at the top of the standings.

(Some nineteenth-century novelties:)

I am the ghost of Fanny Price:
Do you feel, dear Edmund, that acting's quite nice?

I am the ghost of Miss Jane Eyre:
Pick up your feet, man! Look out for the stair!

I am the ghost of Wackford Squeers:
With my son I've struck oil — just look at them tears!

I am the ghosts of Dombey & Son:
It took little Florence to make us as one.

I am the ghost of poor little Esther:
Lady Dedlock looks pale — what can have distressed her?

I am the ghost of discreet Inspector Bucket:
I seem to have lost the trail again, confound it!

I am the ghost of Nelly Dean:
Heathcliff's a devil to know what I mean.

I am the ghost of the squire of the Grange:
Heathcliff's turned up, and my wife's turned so strange!

(Two clerihews:)

Thomas Hardy
Was usually tardy.
The sooner the worse
In this universe.

Edith Sitwell
Didn't write a bit well.
Her verses, sadly,
Stand up badly.

A MORALIST'S ZODIAC

O you who run before the gale
The SCORPION's sting lies in his tail;
He plants his venom to remind
The forward of what lies behind.

The ARCHER is a man of parts;
He launches his unerring darts
At poseur, pedant, prude, and prig,
And anyone who makes it big.

The lecherous GOAT must be retrained:
The fool who lets him go unchained
Draws horns as sharp as Cupid's darts
To his permissive hinderparts.

The MAN WHO BEARS THE WATER-POT
May well be thirsty, but should not
By rash consumption of his wares
Bring down the value of the shares.

The FISH, though paired, cannot agree
On how they may attain the sea.
Which way is upstream? Which is down?
Could they be one on this, they'd drown.

The RAM resolves to have his fling
And wildly capers in the spring.
But in his fervor, like as not,
He breaks a leg, and must be shot.

Of provocation just a shred's
Enough to make the BULL see red.
He rushes forth to wade in gore,
But then he meets the Matador.

Still yoked together go the TWINS.
An apt reminder: when one sins
the other suffers too. They share
A fate that's common, if unfair.

Towards his objects of affection
The CRAB proceeds by indirection,
By sidelong sidlings comes to clinches
And gains their hearts by nips and pinches.

The LION emits a mighty roar
But stays as hungry as before;
His more sagacious mate enjoys
A fuller meal with much less noise.

If sun will shine and wind will blow
This VIRGIN will not long stay so.
Even within this present tense
She has no time for abstinence.

Men, beasts, sea-creatures — strange to see
The SCALES in this menagerie.
They say to horns and claws and stings
There must be balance in all things.

Poems

2000-2005

A REVISED VERSION
for Roger Sale

The wind whirled up into a voice
calling "Abraham!"
He bent his head, he bowed his knee:
"My Lord God, here I am."

"Journey into Moriah;
take with you the one
sacrifice acceptable:
Isaac, your son."

Abraham rose up early,
saddled the ass, and clove
wood for the burnt offering.
Into Moriah he rode

with Isaac his waist embracing
so he need not see that face
sparkling with adventure.
When they reached the place

Abraham and Isaac
together toiled up the slope:
the boy bent almost double
under the wood; the rope,

the whetted knife, and the fire
were a load for Abraham.
The boy said "All is ready,
Father, but where's the lamb

to lay upon the altar
and slaughter?" Abraham sighed.
He fitted one stone to another.
"My son, He will provide."

Rough was the altar, but ready.
Isaac made never a sound,
but the blood drained sharply from his face
when Abraham seized him, bound

his hands behind him, and, lifting
his son up in his arms,
laid him down on the altar.
The air fell tensely calm.

Somewhere a bird called softly.
Slanting through the glade
the first ray of sunlight glinted
on the uplifted blade,

when a voice that gleamed like the sunlight
spoke: "Abraham, hold your hand!"
The brilliant glitter widened,
the topmost boughs were fanned

by a breeze that set the leaves spinning
and as suddenly died away;
down below, in a thicket,
something large, shaggy, grey,

broke into raucous complaining.
There, among the thorns,
a ram stamped its hooves, and bleated,
caught fast by the horns.

And the voice, as the sun struck warmer,
warmly said: "Abraham,
loosen the rope, free Isaac;
take and kill the ram.

I stay the hand, because the heart
proved apt to sacrifice
its lesser love. Come, free the boy,
and let the ram suffice."

As if just that moment awakened
the man his son unbound.
Then turned, and threw; the knife-blade
stuck quivering in the ground.

Clenching his hands on the altar,
Abraham stared at the sky;
a sob caught his breath for an instant,
then, chest heaving, he cried:

"Lord God, who at a glance can scan
the heart's profoundest truth,
what need had you to wring from me
such a conclusive proof?"

He turned, took Isaac by the hand,
they freed the trembling ram;
as the boy stroked its woolly head,
thus spake Abraham:

"Let boulders crush us, fire consume;
savor them as you will.
No blood of mine, to please your taste,
nor any blood I'll spill.

Here stands a beast, and here a child,
and here stands a free man.
Annihilate us all at once:
I don't doubt that you can.

And now I doubt not that you will,
since no more I'll provide
the offering of a slavish heart
to glut a childish pride."

Turning, he took the downward path
leaping from boulder to boulder,
with the ram at his heels, and the laughing child
perched high on his shoulder.

Above them, swift across the clear
dawn sky there swept a flush
that deepened as it spread, till all
the face of heaven blushed.

THE WISE CHILD

What's that noise?
the child by the hearth
demanded.
So curious, so serious,
unlike any lullaby
it sounded.

It's the wind
that sings in the chimney
they answered.
He pondered; he wondered
if only the wind told the truth
uncensored.

Not a song;
no hymn, nor hosanna,
no amen.
Not scary, not eerie,
just otherwise, purely
inhuman.

Not a howl,
nor moan, not a skirl;
no crying.
Not boding, not chiding;
no oracle, no omen
supplying.

Was it God's,
the voice that defied
translation?
Uncaring, unenquiring,
unmoved by any human
condition,

venting mad
soliloquies now and
forever?
Then praying, and praising
were mere wind also: infancy
was over.

SIMPLE SOULS
for Steve Buttle

When first our crosstrees
nicked their horizon, they hailed
us as blessings.

When our keels grated
aground, great gouges
branding the earth, they took
us for angels.

When some of us hoisted our muskets
they coughed: huge birds
plumped to the ground, scrambling feathers
flummoxed with blood. How they whooped,
applauding our aims!

When we upped our figure —
spreadeagled, splayed, through each palm
the nails gritting, sinews contorted,
the rack of the ribs heartwrenching —
their jaws slumped; their eyes shrank; they knew
we meant business.

CAPITAL

(Matthew 25, 14-30)
for Margaret Drabble

The man with a single talent —
when his Lord had upped and gone —
sat down to take stock of his talents
and, finding he had but one
(so what would he do if he lost it?)
buried it like a bone.

The fellow who had five talents
and even the fellow with two
aggressively set out to make much
of what their talents could do
(and what if one talent were squandered?
They still had a residue).

But, in the event, they prospered
as surely they'd sensed that they would.
When their Lord returned, they accounted
for the killings they'd made. He said "Good
and faithful servants…": his moral
universally understood.

But the man with the single talent,
who had hidden it deep beneath
a talentless demeanor
(but surely he was no thief?)
was cast into outer darkness
where there's weeping and gnashing of teeth..

And his solitary talent was gifted
to the slickest profiteer;
with him, it increases in interest
a thousand-fold every year:
it's sinful to fear for one's talent
when that talent is something to fear.

FAMILY MATTERS
for Ruth

The sunlight touches up the frame that holds them
remote and radiant in their wedding clothes,
and sets the orange of a still life flaring;
fresh coffee gobbles on the stove

and he feels ten years younger. Almost-forgotten
dulcet Italian words well to his lips:
soave, semplice... Their little daughter
wades to the table, topples, grips

her mother's skirt, and with a brief loud comment
bares one sun-spattered thigh clear to the hip.
As Mother bends, garners the small blonde head,
her eyes meet his, and say — though nothing's said —
there's no recovery, just brief agreement
what's left to cherish, what is past lament.

Today, at least, may turn out not inclement.

BOY IN A CANOE

The water weighs him in the palm
of an appraising hand;
juggles, like a lucky charm,
the bright blue shell
to veer its bouncy prow away from land

and my restraints. I do try not to quack.
He's safely wedged:
yellow lifejacket, grin, damp mop
of fledge perked up,
cocky, he rides the slick

swells, starts to take his licks,
setting a cracking pace, but soon,
smoother, controlled,
his paddle pans the water,
comes up gold.

He makes her fast himself, then risks
my hand again, chats up our confidence —
young salt, my little whisker —
as we trudge back the beach, each crunch asserting
shared strides, and this new footing.

A PRELUDE
for John Steane

*Ah, my daughter, it is easy to see that your forebears have
economised for you. Through the long ages they have sat mutely
by their firesides, spinning and weaving through the quiet hours.
Your song is made of their silences.*
– Emma Calvé's father, quoted in her autobiography
and by J.B. Steane in *The Grand Tradition*.

An old familiar setting, *sotto voce*;
A tiny steady burble from the lamp,
Clock chips away the hours, the fire composes.

Mother's chapped fingers flicker round her needle;
Father sustains his newspaper, blunt type
swells through thick glasses to absorb the eyes

that she inherits. Grandad mouths a hole
for breath to eddy through, if it still choose.
Dog's crooked his paws to cupboard up his nose.

Nobody's said a word for simply ages.
Close-knit, tight-fisted, they will hold their peace
in trust for her, until the breath they've saved

inspires a new sensation in great cities:
diva bravissima, last word in *derniers cris*...
Here is the prelude. Dreamily, she touches
a throat bejeweled by long economies.

DEALING WITH DAD
for Jonathan Raban

Night after night, I watched you play
game after game, in overlays
of black and red.
This did not leave you much to say.
Your last-born, I was bred
to just your style of shuffling. Now
the petty cheats that you'ld allow
I've inherited.

Killing time still clicks
its tongue at jacks
that need their queens; elusive aces.
It never stops
hinting at vacant spaces
cheap fillings won't disguise,
bound to attract censorious eyes,
pursed lips, averted faces.

Was this your teaching? Well, you're long past blame.
Besides, we used to call the game
Patience, back then, back there.
You knew it by no other name.
For me, now, *Solitaire*
sums up a kinds of recreation.
A minor point: for fuller implications
I don't much care.

HOBGOBLINS
(Or, homage to J*hn *shbery)

The point is that they didn't like you much
on that first meeting, at the Russian joint
among the bougainvilleas. No eye-witnesses,
but one could argue that it had to do
with shreds of tapioca, Haydn's Seventh Mass —
those, and the scent of cumin in the air.

They hadn't had malaria, so they knew
what came between the cufflinks and the qualm,
or — take a different tack — if Fra Angelico
had been to Sydney, he'd have been so bronzed
that not one velvet peccadillo would have grinned
at his accountants. I'd say you need a drink.

Did someone once mistake you for James Bond
behind the sixth-floor elevator at the Bon?
Tell her it's just God's snot. But incubi
play ping-pong all night long; they heave deep sighs,
deep as that bathrobe of deep apricot.
Remember not to scratch. And that's the point.

SODMARSH

The vale drags down a blind of frigid
rain from the mist-scarfed ridges;
the waters rise to suckle at the bridges.

Here's land that masticates a grudge
against its tenants. Thorns spike the hedge.
Cows lie in their muck and will not budge.

Rain floods the furrows that the slow plough dredges,
and flays the ploughman's cheeks; a sucking sludge
strives to tug off the boots that strive to trudge.

Spring arrives late, and nothing really alters:
the thin beer sours; the dunghills buzz and swelter;
the cesspools belch as they extend their cultures.

Blotches of ugly chutney clog the sedges.
On skinny boughs a dingy frogspawn lodges.
The sun goes down behind a sieve of midges.

Neighbors

MARY JENNINGS

A leprosy blanched all at once
and, for a month or so,
we blinked to meet her, all that sleek
raven transformed to snow.
And yet her smile was just the same
or, if not quite, the change
hinted a glint of jauntiness,
a candid mischief. Strange:
it dawned on us as simply as
it came to grow on her —
a lightness concentrated on
accomplished drifts of hair.

WALTER GREEN: DEAD IN SPRINGTIME

She: I strolled by Walter Green's, looked round the yard:
       barely a fortnight gone, yet all his trees
       have burst themselves to bloom. How he'd have loved to see
       spring's suddenness again. It seems so hard.

He: You think so? I'd have guessed Walt's time of year
       fell later on. All this froth, floss, and thrusting
       extravagance he'd find a mite disgusting,
       prefer how fall makes hard facts stand out clear.

She: You could be right. Flowering was not Walt's thing;
       he might not even notice spring had come!

He: That's a bit much. Walt's not entirely dumb.
       I'd say he chose not to be swayed by spring.
       And there's the pity: now he has no choice.

She: I hate it when you use that *knowing* voice.

ZOE TEODAKIS

She is a serious one. Quick to detect
pedantic fudge, she wrinkles up her nose;
she wants to exercize her intellect

so it may strut. Scarlet, she paints her toes,
matching the cover of the *War and Peace*
she's annotated. She'll scratch her ear, expose

a slim black bra-strap, then release
a sudden volley of delighted praise —
perhaps excessive — for *Don Juan.* Greece

is where she'll be next spring. Or so she prays.
she could cause havoc in the Academies
with novel slants on Sappho, with displays

of such neat ankles, and such earnest eyes.

JACK BULLARD

He's in his yard. I call *Good morning, Jack!*
to see his face become all razor-burn
around hot eyes, and make him turn,
implacably, a rusty-sweatered back

rigid with indignation. What is it about me
that gets his goat? Nobody seems to know:
it's just my fancy, it's not really so.
In any case, it's just his way: *Oh, he's*

a real character, is Jack. Oh, is he? So,
I'll sketch a skit, and make of him a star.
It will be very funny when his car
won't start, and then explodes. Then let him glow

with outrage on his sooty mug, his hair
singed to a crisp. You'll die with laughter
to see him prancing, cursing after
the rake leaps up to smash his nose. Prepare

for mirth, when Jack is plagued with boils
and can't quit scratching that red meaty neck
until his hands are bound, and crows come peck
those bulbous eyes. A squirt of scalding oil

will spice the comedy. He'll be so surprised
when his house crumbles round him, so we spy
Jack crouching in the john. I go too far? But why
can't the old bastard act more civilized?

9/11

Of course…

But bear in mind, too, the honeymoon couple
who spent all day in bed:
for half the time were outrageously active;
for half, slept like the dead.

Collapsed on the floor lay a welter of clothing
and toppled shoes:
having no mind to suffer the television
they blissfully missed the news.

MEET THE CANDIDATE

He is the man
whose teeth are gleaming,
whose eyes are counters,
whose hands are glad.

Set his face
against your grievance:
his heart will swell,
nor will he shrink.

His be the voice
of your good reason;
his means such ends
as you believe in.

Digest him well.
Lend him your ears.
Let him be party
to your breathing.

Let him be putty
in your hands,
that hardens:
Let him press your flesh.

O SAY CAN YOU SEE
for Hugh Brogan

None of my British business, you may say,
go stuff yourself with your own Union Jack!
Okay: it's not my flag. I'm not a caretaker.
Still, when the tall pole creaks I glance to see it
garish against the dark clouds racing, in such a fix
someone should ease it down. Whose business is it,
when the wind freshens as it veers around
and canvas answers with a hollow clap
to thunder in the air?
                    The colors thresh
and foam, a flummoxed galaxy
and tumbling stripes confounded. Someone must hear
those highstrung twangs, the strums and bangs that mount
a fusillade, as if this ensign aimed to
shoot its way out, or bomblike burst in air.
These things cost more than money.
                              How long can it sustain
the smacks it deals itself, a gale that cracks
Old Glory like a whiplash overhead?
There must be someone who is paid to see
it doesn't rip to shreds.....
                    Hell, I should care.
It's not my bloody country, anyway.

IN THE FRARI: A NOCTURNAL
for Peter Porter

Brick bulwarks shutter out the glare;
the hordes and hubbub everywhere
San Marco's cross beast bares his teeth. Oh,

who cares for Titian, anyway?
But who would not be charmed to spy
how, with despondent handkerchief,

this small lion weeps so sore to see
Canova's slipped into his tomb
but left the door ajar,

while four huge Moors strain every thew,
rolling starched eyeballs, to sustain
the pride of Pesaro?

You'd like to think that, when night falls,
and the tall doors are locked and barred,
the lion curls into a ball and

smirking, snoozes. With great care
the Moors set down their burden,
mop off sweat, stretch, yawn, and share a

joke, a jigger of Bacardi,
as, from the nook that hoards the bones
of Claudio Monteverdi

a rill of music starts to well:
a tiny cobweb fanfare will
launch the faint wash of choristers

that slims away into the merest
wisp, when seeps of dawn call Moors
and lion to resume their poses

and edify new troupes of tourists.

IL RITORNO D'ULISSE IN PATRIA

Mi' vecia
Zanni calls his wife;
sharp eyes, rankling wrinkles.

Also his boat;
her paint in blisters,
hiccoughing motor.

Also his old accoutred mistress;
roofs, aerials, slanting *campanili*
spread out before him, on the long haul home
from San Michele.

RIO TERÀ DEI PENSIERI

The slop of water from a bucket dons
a furry dustcoat, picks up chips
for gondolas, then sidles
to where the pavement's cracked — and then it's gone:
what trail it leaves the sun soon sponges up.
That's all there is to irrigate an idle
choked-up, filled-in, paved-over stream of thoughts.

People must live in these drab houses, but
the one apparent lodger lolls and bakes
atop the wall you keep your distance from,
by fixed decree. He scratches, spits, chain-smokes
fascisti. And he sports a gun,
the blunt accessory to boredom's flat
choked-up, filled-in, paved-over stream of thoughts.

Who would come here, if law were not enforced?
Nothing to view, to snapshoot, or research;
no bar, *gelateria*, vendors' carts.
What's now a prison used to be a church:
now, there's a change. How aptly such
stilted translation speaks for this inert
choked-up, filled-in, paved-over stream of thoughts.

DAY OF RECKONING

Rather too old to be computer-savvy,
He uses — always has — an abacus.
White-robed, wool-bearded, the old lovey-dovey
calls you to watch. Divinely, digits shuttle
beads along wires. Snow-whites are virtuous,
but all too scanty, set against the total
that mounts, of damnably bright scarlet
beans that build row on row, and carry
over, implacably. All you can say is *Sorry*.
And so am I, He nods, and down you go
into the flames that sear, and yet devour not,
eternally, eternally. That means forever.
Mightn't the sentence be a mite excessive
however long you've sinned, however massive your
evil accumulation? It does seem odd:
He seemed a nice enough old fart, did God?
You called him "just", and "merciful", the sod?

AFTERLIVES

Perhaps you get what you believe in. Some
flit up to paradise,
where all the tears are wiped away, and
everything's very nice.

Those who insist on nothing less
will find their hell; only themselves to blame
for wilful wretchedness.

some will resume the earth, and take the air
in endless variations,
born-again perishers.

I aim to be surprised at feeling
incredibly fatigued. I'll yawn
and go to sleep, unwittingly assured
of the tomorrow that will never dawn.

THE DOWNPOUR

Sleep will not come. He keeps his eyes
trained on the ceiling that he cannot see
and pays heed to the darkness. On the roof
the rain is typing his biography.

How it taps on, and on! Taking dictation
at the wind's will, insufferably it hammers
away at all the commas that prolong one
long lifetime sentence to a constant stammer

that's sometimes moved to desperate fits and flurries,
then sullenly lulls back to the dull pounding —
out of narrative humdrum and numbskull.
When will it ever end? What chance of rounding —

off a tale so sodden, soggy, so banal?
All wasted energy, diffuse, damp, incomplete…
He wants it just to stop. His best hope is
rain too must have a deadline it must meet.

A FAMILY ALBUM

Now this is my Mum — the lady in black,
And here's all the family gathered at home;
And this one is Albert, who never came back.

Hello! Cousin Charlie — but he got the sack.
Behold Aphrodite sprung out of the foam!
And this is my Mum — the lady in black.

This here is our church, where they put up the plaque.
Oh goodness, my hair could do with a comb!
And this one's our Albert, who never came back.

Here he's in uniform, rifle and pack;
and here's the nice card Jane sent us from Rome;
Doesn't Mum look really *distingueé* in black?

Here's the troop-train, about to puff off down the track.
St. Paul's — what a view from the top of the dome!
Albert's third from the left: he never came back.

Tommy. Aunt Enid (the dog was called Jack).
And old Mr. Cuttle — he looks like a gnome.
You can barely see Mum, but she's there, in her black,
right next to our Albert, who never came back.

THE PROMISED LAND

It takes the purest, most pellucid day
to let one see how, miles on miles away,
beyond the known hills far across the bay,

outlines far loftier range. It does one proud
to hail as mountain what might yet be cloud,
no sooner ascertained than disavowed,

sparking high hopes uncertified by maps,
desires that no theodolite entraps,
whose lengths and latitudes rhyme with Perhaps...

there could be altitudes where spirits move
through winter palaces, through crystal groves,
peaceable kingdoms, protectorates of love?

Yes, but beyond the grasp of crude insistence:
remoteness is the nth power of resistance.
They keep their promise as they keep their distance,

quite inaccessible, except as token
expansive vows are indistinctly spoken,
those unfulfilled as yet remain unbroken.

ACKNOWLEDGEMENTS

Many people have contributed to the making of this book: it has been a labor of love and of friendship on all their parts. Without their generous support and commitment, this project might have languished long. Especial thanks go first to William's nephew Neil Dunlop for unearthing that tattered notebook and sending it on; to his niece Katharine Andrews for permission to use her "Asphodel" (a picture he greatly admired) on the cover; to Gavin Andrews and Tom Marshall for their work in creating a forthcoming web site. And a great thanks to Hugh Brogan for allowing his sprats to see the light of day!

Samantha Paxton, Sarah Lysons, Zaid Al-Farisi and Joshua Large did most of the leg-work in getting things together: their tireless typing, scanning, burning and general technological expertise kept the ball rolling smoothly. Josh deserves special mention for so ably deciphering the juvenilia.

My greatest debt, however, is to William's friend and colleague Roger Sale. His devotion to this effort — his unfailing support, patience, advice, and, above all, energy — has pushed our project to completion.

Many others, hearing of our work, wanted to help finance publication. Below are the names of those who gave so generously of their dollars and their pounds. To all, my heartfelt thanks.

Erik Abbott &
Kate Dunlop

Dennis & Maria Andrews

Brian Bailey

Linda Bierds &
Sydney Kaplan

Jack & Midge Brenner

David & Joyce Brewster

Hugh Brogan

Blair Burroughs

Marion Codd, Max & Kate

Julian Cotton

Theo & Goodwin Deacon

Mike Dillon

Margaret Drabble

Miranda Dunlop

Peter Dunlop &
Penelope Rose

Ruth Dunlop

Richard Dunn

David C. Fowler

Malcolm Griffith

Ran Hennes

Richard Kenney

Michael Kern

Eric La Guardia

Alan Lawrence

Richard Lindley &
Carole Stone

Thomas Lockwood

Jacque Lysons

Thomas Marshall &
Dana Shiller

Paola Martini-Scott

David McCracken

David & Gracia McGovern

Otto Reinert &
Pat Hurshell

Roger & Dorothy Sale

Frances Spooner

Rae Tufts

Kay Vail-Hayden

John Webster

Jason West &
Ioana Dima

Jim Whitson &
Patricia Adams

Douglas & Teresa Willard

Susan Williams

From the late 1950s through the early '70s, William Dunlop was widely regarded as one of Britain's most promising young poets. While an undergraduate at Cambridge, he published in *Granta* (which he also edited for a time), *Cambridge Opinion, Delta, Prospect,*and *Universities Poetry*, a prestigious launching pad for student poets heading for a literary career.

In Memorium
William Dunlop, 1936-2005

It was via *Universities Poetry* that William came to the United States. In late January 1961, a poetry reading was held at the Crown & Greyhound, a pub in Dulwich, south-east London. The American Theodore Roethke had top billing; William and several other young poets whom they had published shared supporting roles. Roethke was so taken with William's work that he immediately recruited him for the University of Washington in Seattle — where in 1962 he began to teach writing and literature.

He published, occasionally, in *The New Statesman, The London Magazine, Encounter, Poetry Northwest,* and *Cambridge Review*. In 1973-1974 — a very productive sabbatical year — publishers took notice. Oxford University Press planned to publish his first collection. Considerable dispute arose, however, as to which poems would be included and which not. It ended in a frustrating stalemate and no book appeared. An offer from Gollancz to be one of a "Poetry Quintet" was later declined.

So began a long (over 20 years) poetic silence. A silence filled, however, with his voice in other writing — essays, sports journalism, reviews of books, of films, but most notably of operas and recitals and recordings for both local and national publications. And filled with his teaching voice — he continued to teach with distinction in Seattle until 2001.

Only after came the new flowering of poetic energy.

Note from Rose Alley Press

I am delighted to see more of William Dunlop's poetry in print. In 1977, as a senior at the University of Washington, I took a verse writing class from William, and visited him periodically after that. In 1990, having started a small press, I twice asked him for the opportunity to publish his poems. He twice refused. In 1995, I started a new company, Rose Alley Press. In the summer of 1996, I wrote him a long letter, trying one last time to persuade him to let me publish his work. A month later, he phoned me and agreed to my proposal.

I was thrilled that after nearly two decades of feeling that William's verse had been undervalued, I could help redress the injustice. The next eight months saw fastidious attention paid to ordering, editing, computer typesetting, and printing the poems we had chosen, as well as designing the book's cover. Finally, on June 17th, 1997, *Caruso for the Children & Other Poems* was published. It was popular upon release, and it remains so — indeed it is Rose Alley's best-selling title. I am overjoyed that more of his magnificently crafted verse will reach appreciative readers. I wish all involved in this new publication the very best.

David D. Horowitz
Rose Alley Press

INDEX OF FIRST LINES